INCARCERATION AND OLDER WOMEN
Giving Back Not Giving Up

Regina White Benedict

Edited by
Lois Presser and Beth Easterling

First published in Great Britain in 2025 by

Bristol University Press
University of Bristol
1-9 Old Park Hill
Bristol
BS2 8BB
UK
t: +44 (0)117 374 6645
e: bup-info@bristol.ac.uk

Details of international sales and distribution partners are available at bristoluniversitypress.co.uk

© Bristol University Press 2025

British Library Cataloguing in Publication Data
A catalogue record for this book is available from the British Library

ISBN 978-1-5292-3161-8 hardcover
ISBN 978-1-5292-3165-6 paperback
ISBN 978-1-5292-3167-0 ePub
ISBN 978-1-5292-3168-7 ePdf

The right of Regina White Benedict to be identified as author and of Lois Presser and Beth Easterling as editors of this work has been asserted by them in accordance with the Copyright, Designs and Patents Act 1988.

All rights reserved: no part of this publication may be reproduced, stored in a retrieval system, or transmitted in any form or by any means, electronic, mechanical, photocopying, recording, or otherwise without the prior permission of Bristol University Press.

Every reasonable effort has been made to obtain permission to reproduce copyrighted material. If, however, anyone knows of an oversight, please contact the publisher.

The statements and opinions contained within this publication are solely those of the author and editors and not of the University of Bristol or Bristol University Press. The University of Bristol and Bristol University Press disclaim responsibility for any injury to persons or property resulting from any material published in this publication.

Bristol University Press works to counter discrimination on grounds of gender, race, disability, age and sexuality.

Cover design: Hannah Gaskamp
Front cover image: getty/ annedala

Contents

Foreword by Lois Presser		iv
Preface		vii
1	Ageing Less Than Gracefully	1
2	Welcome to My Home: Cell Block D	10
3	Older, Wiser, and Incarcerated	27
4	A Positively Negative Experience	37
5	Parenting Behind Bars	52
6	Ageing in Their Own Words: Peace of Mind, Body, and Circumstances	71
7	'Usefulness' of a 'Useless' Population	89
8	Why Not Give Them a Chance?	104
Afterword by Beth Easterling and Lois Presser		110
Appendix A: Sample Demographics and Details of Current Sentence		114
Appendix B: Research Synopsis		116
Appendix C: Suggestions for Further Reading		117
References		119
Index		131

Foreword

Lois Presser

In bleak and uncertain times, good stories are crucial. Good stories motivate people to meet current challenges and endure difficult conditions. They endow challenges and conditions with meaning. Victor Frankl (1984) describes 'the human capacity to creatively turn life's negative aspects into something positive or constructive' (p 139). Frankl's own suffering and loss during the Holocaust anchor his argument that 'what matters is to make the best of any given situation' (Frankl, 1984). His psychotherapeutic programme, logotherapy, was designed to help clients find meaning whatever their circumstances.

The mostly older people in prison whom Gina Benedict interviewed at the Kentucky Correctional Institution for Women made positive meaning of their circumstances. They told stories of lending support. Specifically, they described helping, now and in future, younger generations – fellow women in prison, family members outside of the prison, and hypothetical others. These stories were about care and better lives. Gina understood these stories as reflecting an impulse toward generativity, or 'the concern in establishing and guiding the next generation', which Erikson (1963/1950) deemed an 'essential' stage of human development (p 267).

This redemptive line of thinking – finding the good in the bad – could be dangerous. It could encourage going along with injustice, akin to Merton's (1938) ritualism. It might even put a positive slant on ill-treatment and suffering, both in the past and present, including that which the individual herself caused. Consequently, it could discourage resistance and accountability. It is hard to reconcile these possibilities with critical, abolitionist criminology.

Notwithstanding such cautions, however, I would insist that the good stories people who are incarcerated tell, matter for justice. First, to be able to anticipate better things from a subjugated position suggests that subjugation is not complete. Second, to be able to do good things as a designated criminal counters the characterization of 'criminals' as selfish and corrupt. Finally, to construct a decent identity when evidence of past indecency abounds, may yet provoke lasting personal change (O'Connor, 2000).

To concern ourselves with the good stories that people in prison tell is to centre them as actors, however much their agency is constrained. In contrast, to the extent that prisons (and other carceral facilities) are designed to do good, the 'doing' casts the institution and its staff in lead roles, with 'clients' as beneficiaries/targets. Those institutional efforts, not surprisingly, orient to system objectives – to increase order and reduce recidivism. Criminologists likewise mainly ask whether convicts are achieving rehabilitation and, later, reintegration, but rarely whether they are achieving what they want to achieve (cf. Ward and Maruna, 2007). Prison researchers traditionally ask how people in prison cope or adapt to their punishing circumstances. But generativity is not the same thing as coping or adapting (see Kazemian, 2021). It is not about getting along; it is about fostering good in the world. It is indelibly social and creative.

Gina passed away in 2021 at 44, the same age as Evelyn (a pseudonym) when she and Gina met. Evelyn was serving a 70-year sentence for murder and attempted murder. She had recently learned that she would not be considered for parole for another 20 years. But Evelyn worked hard on personal growth while in prison and looked ahead to the contributions she might one day make: "I think I'll be a good influence when I get out, even if I'm 100 years old. I've set a goal. I'll do it." How could paradigms centred on adaptation, coping, or even resilience in prison, and desistance and reintegration afterwards, adequately capture Evelyn's outlook and resolve to make a difference in her lifetime? They could not.

The chapters of this book illuminate imposed hardships, affronts to autonomy and health, needs created and unmet, *and* good deeds and compassionate ambitions. The three chapters that review scholarly studies on incarceration, ageing, and generativity, respectively (Chapters 2, 3, and 4) inform three chapters on the women's social experiences across the temporal boundary of one's current sentence and the physical boundary of the prison (Chapters 6, 7, and 8). In their words, we come to understand that prison and ageing hastened by imprisonment can pose formidable challenges it but cannot keep its subjects from telling stories of meaningful lives of furthering shared well-being.

References

Erikson, Erik H. 1963 (1950). *Childhood and Society*, 2nd Ed. New York: W.W. Norton & Co.

Frankl, V. E. 1984. *Man's Search for Meaning: An Introduction to Logotherapy*, 3rd Ed. New York: Touchstone.

Kazemian, L. 2021. *Positive Growth and Redemption in Prison: Finding Light Behind Bars and Beyond*. Abingdon: Routledge.

Merton, R. K. 1938. 'Social Structure and Anomie'. *American Sociological Review*, 3: 672–682.

O'Connor, P. E. 2000. *Speaking of Crime: Narratives of Prisoners*. Lincoln, NE and London: University of Nebraska Press.

Ward, T. & S. Maruna. 2007. *Rehabilitation: Beyond the Risk Paradigm*. London and New York: Routledge.

Preface

Dr. Regina (Gina) White Benedict passed away at the age of 44 on the 31st of March, 2021.

She was Assistant Professor of Criminal Justice and Coordinator of the Criminal Justice programme at Maryville College in Maryville, Tennessee. She earned her PhD in Sociology from the University of Tennessee in 2009. She earned her MA degree from East Tennessee State University (2000) and BA from Mississippi State University (1998). Among the honours she received were a Most Distinguished Graduate Student award from East Tennessee State University and an Excellence in Teaching award from the University of Tennessee. The editors of this book have prepared Gina's doctoral dissertation, *Giving Back Not Giving Up: Generativity Among Older Female Inmates* for this book publication. They have not reframed or restructured the dissertation and have minimally edited Gina's words.

1

Ageing Less Than Gracefully

Research on people in prison tends to focus on the negative aspects of incarceration, and rightly so as few would deny that incarceration is largely a negative experience. Studies of ageing likewise amass evidence that the process of ageing is challenging, if not necessarily and uniformly aversive. These two social realities – imprisonment and ageing – merge where a relatively small but growing subgroup of the population is concerned – older people in prison. We have hardly heard from this group.[1]

The prison population is ageing at a concerning rate in the United States and other countries including England, Wales, Scotland, and Japan (Penal Reform International, 2021). In the US, from 1999 to 2016, the number of persons aged 55 and older in state and federal prisons grew by a remarkable 280 per cent while the number of their younger counterparts increased by just 3 per cent (McKillop and Boucher, 2018). Analysts project that by the year 2030, as many as one in three people in US prisons will be 50 years of age or older (Nellis, 2022).

Several factors appear to explain these increases. They reflect a rise in new admissions for serious crime as well as sentencing laws enacted in the past several decades, including laws requiring lengthy and determinate sentences for violent offences and substance abuse. The increases can also be traced to the abolition of parole in some states. Whatever sentencing reforms have recently been implemented, past and present structures have had the inevitable effect of warehousing large numbers of older people, many of whom face long sentences.

People who are incarcerated, like their mainstream counterparts, are prone to more physical problems as they age. Compared with young people in prison, older people who are incarcerated are more susceptible to both minor and chronic physical illnesses and suffer from higher levels of mental illness (Davoren et al, 2015; Haesen et al, 2019; Solares et al, 2020). They are at higher risk of contracting urinary tract infections, gastrointestinal infections, hepatitis, and pneumonia (Falter, 1999; Aday, 2003) and higher frequency of use of medical services (Lindquist and Lindquist, 1999). Compared with older people outside of prison, those who are incarcerated are disproportionately affected by inadequate medical care, past and present, and by prior alcohol and drug abuse (Rikard and Rosenberg, 2007).

Notwithstanding these gloomy findings, ageing also yields positive outcomes. Age may exacerbate the harms of imprisonment, but it might bring wisdom or other, hardly considered resources. This book is concerned with how older women who are incarcerated themselves experience ageing in the carceral setting and how they furthermore make meaning behind bars, finding and creating opportunities to experience grace and to do good.

Generativity and ageing women in prison

Generativity, a term coined by psychologist Erik Erikson (1950), is a commitment to the larger society and its continuation and/or improvement through the next generation. In other words, generativity is 'giving back'. I explore generativity behind bars, particularly generativity among older women behind bars. Given gendered circumstances and experiences, how do they make meaning and derive purpose from imprisonment? I draw on in-depth interviews with women incarcerated in Kentucky to illuminate their generative desires and how they fulfil these desires behind bars. Above all, this book tells a story of resistance – of the human capacity to make meaning under the direst of circumstances.

While prison is a sombre environment, older people endure many years of incarceration full of both pain *and* pleasure. Prior research primarily concentrates on negative aspects of incarceration, such as family separation, mental illness, victimization, and trauma. The positives, while arguably fewer in number, are largely ignored. Generativity, or giving back to others, offers benefits for both the person who is incarcerated and society, but opportunities to be generative are limited in prison. Still, people who are incarcerated can find innovative ways to be generative while behind bars. Prior research (for example, Kashy and Morash, 2022) points to the contribution that self-efficacy and education make to self-reported generativity among women in prison. Exploring such correlations for all groups of women helps to more comprehensively explore ways to support the well-being during the incarceration period and can potentially lower recidivism rates.

The concept of generativity encompasses both desires and behaviours intended to improve the next generation. Generative adults ponder the legacy they will leave behind. Yet it would seem likely that, due to incarceration, people in prison would not express generativity to the same degree or in the same way as people outside of prison. Indeed, fear, of dying in prison, and preoccupation with daily affronts would seem more paramount (Aday, 2006). Nor, however, can we take for granted that older people in prison do not share the more transcendent aspirations associated with generativity.

Ageing women and the prison experience

Women have been a growing segment of the incarcerated population in the United States over the past several decades, even as imprisonment rates generally have declined (Heimer et al, 2022), with almost five times as many women in a US prison in 2020 than there were in 1980 (The Sentencing Project, 2022). Sawyer (2018) observes, 'While recent reforms have reduced the total number of people in state prisons since 2009, almost all of the decrease has been among men.' Dholakia (2021) thus writes, 'It's clear that decarceration efforts are leaving women behind.'

White-haired women stooped or in wheelchairs are not the 'typical' image associated with women in prison. However, such is the growing reality in many US prisons today. According to the Bureau of Justice Statistics, in 2019, the percentage of persons aged 40 and older among women in prison in 2019 was 37.5 per cent, and 8.3 per cent of them were 55 and older (Carson, 2020). These women have children who are grown and on their own. Typically, this stage in life brings retirement, vacations, and grandchildren. For older women in prison, daily life is experienced quite differently from their counterparts in free society.[2] Their position in the prison social order is significant and their experience of incarceration is unique, yet older women in prison are generally considered a small and trivial part of the prison population. Therefore, very little is known about their prison adjustment, hardships, and achievements. It should not be assumed that older women who are incarcerated share the same experiences as younger age groups. Older incarcerated women are often mothers of older children, and grandmothers, perhaps even great-grandmothers, to children that they may never have met.

While previous research has explored the challenges posed by incarceration for motherhood (see Baubach, 1985; Watterson, 1996; Enos, 2001; Sharp and Marcus-Mendoza, 2001; Belknap, 2007; Easterling, Presser, and Feldmeyer, 2021), with few exceptions (for example, Dressel and Barnhill, 1994; Krabill and Aday, 2005) scholars have paid far less attention to the effects of incarceration on the relationships older women have with *adult* children and grandchildren. Even short periods of separation severely compromise the daily functioning of families with young children, but older people who are incarcerated often have adult children who have lived independently of their mothers, perhaps with children of their own. Separation is arguably not as detrimental to the well-being of the family unit as with younger women with young children. Older women must also adjust to family separation, but they may do so differently than younger women. We know little about this type of adjustment.

Prior studies of ageing in prison tend to focus on issues of physical and mental health (Genders and Player, 1990; Koenig, Johnson, Bellard, Denker, and Fenlon, 1995; Aday and Nation, 2001; Aday, 2001) or family visitation (Wikberg and Foster, 1989; Aday, 1995; Aday, 2003). Little attention has been paid to ageing, if not well, then adaptively and meaningfully in prison, though recent research has begun to explore this 'sort' of prison experience for ageing individuals (Maschi and Morgen, 2020; Humblet, 2021), including ageing women (Aday, Krabill, and Deaton-Owens, 2004; Wahidin, 2004; Aday and Krabill, 2011; Handtke et al, 2015; Aday and Dye, 2018).

All people who are incarcerated go through a similar prisonization or adaptation process, but not all of them experience every aspect of it (Girshick, 1999). Plausibly, older people have different needs than younger people in prison; therefore, they are likely to experience prison differently. Larson and Nelson (1984) found that the length of sentence and time already served had a significant impact on adaptation to prison. People who had served more time were better adjusted to the prison environment. For many long-termers, incarceration occasioned a journey of self-discovery.

Older women who are incarcerated represent a thorough-going form of marginalization. Most modern societies still hold to forms of age and gender stratification. Aged members of society are not revered for their experiences or abilities, but rather cast aside to make room for younger members to take over, and women continue to make less money than men in general. In some social circles, women are still referred to as 'the weaker sex'. Women who do not fulfil circumscribed nurturing roles are subject to shame and contempt. In scholarly research, girls and women have traditionally been an afterthought. Likewise, research on people in prison has tended to neglect older individuals. In general, people who are incarcerated, while enjoying a good deal of attention in criminological research, are not of much concern to free society (beyond entertainment, fictionalized or through 'reality' television in pop culture). Incarceration allows 'us' to quite literally remove 'undesirables' not only from our sight but also our minds. Taking all these considerations together, older women in prison are the least likely to receive attention. Their unique needs have hardly been examined.

It is at the intersection of these three social categories – gender, age, and incarceration – that older women who are incarcerated reside. Indeed, we can add more layers of disdain. Women in prison are predominantly from lower-income neighbourhoods; they are disproportionately members of ethnic minorities; they disproportionately suffer from physical disabilities. These women cue all that is ugly and unjust in our society. We may slam the cell door between us and them, walk through the front gate, and pretend that they do not matter, but once you know they are there, once you hear their stories, and once you enter their world, it is my hope that you will take notice and treat them according to their belonging to our one true universal category: that of being human.

The current study

I entered the gates of the Kentucky Correctional Institution for Women, or Pewee Valley as it is often called, in December of 2008. I conducted interviews with 29 women[3] who lived there. Twenty-six of those I interviewed were 40 and older; three were aged 27 to 39. Nine of the women described themselves as Black; 20 described themselves as White. (See Appendix A for a demographic profile with information on conviction and sentence.)

I chose to conduct qualitative interviews in order to give a voice to this small but unique population. I took an exploratory approach and invited the women to discuss issues that were important to them. During most of the interviews, I shared with participants that I am a mother of two young girls. Motherhood provided a basis for relating and thus prompted dialogue. My research participants were eager to talk about their children or grandchildren. One woman stated, "I plan to spoil them [grandchildren] when I get out." I shared that my children were spoiled by their grandparents. The woman smiled and expressed her desire to be with her family and to cook for them on holidays.

By and large, the women I interviewed were vastly different from me. They had borne hardships that I had not encountered. The women in my sample were mostly White (20 women) though disproportionately Black (9 women) relative to the general population of the United States; I am White. Most of the women in the sample were disenfranchised, socially and economically, before they came to prison, which accords with other literature on people in prison.

By design, most of the sample were aged 40 or older. Sontag (1975) suggests that while the prestige of youth affects women and men in similar ways, getting old is more profoundly troublesome for women. Once past menopause, women are more likely to be degraded and discounted than their male counterparts, in various contexts. The adverse impact of ageing on women is tied to the perception that older people are not physically attractive and not vital. Physical attractiveness is more often associated with youthful appearance for women than is the case for men. The social worth of women has been more closely linked with their physical appearance compared to men. It would seem that women lose their social value simply by growing old, whereas older men are more likely to be valued and rewarded for what they do, no matter their age (Hatch, 2005).

In general, my research participants did not discuss difficulties in relation to their age unless with a direct prompt to do so, such as, "What is it like to age in prison?" The typical response was that ageing in prison was not good. They mentioned health problems and required medications, but for most of them being incarcerated at their age was an embarrassment. Peggy, a 58-year-old White woman serving 12 years for trafficking a controlled substance, said, "I didn't realize how old I was until I was in prison. I'm upset being here. This is not where you want to be when you're older." Another woman commented that she never thought she would retire to Pewee Valley (the location of the prison). There was a disconnect between the lives the women imagined for themselves in middle to old age and their present ones.

While both men and women in prison are expected to submit to the institutional authorities and rules, submission seems to be more rigorously enforced in women's prisons. In a study of Texas prisons, McClellan (1994) found that minor occurrences, such as talking in line and failing to eat all of the food on their plates, resulted in citations or punishment for women but never in men's prisons. In effect, women's prison policies have been found to treat women like children. Furthermore, prisons routinely demoralize incarcerated women who already have a high prevalence of histories of sexual abuse. Incarcerated women are given little control over their bodies, from being strip searched in the presence of male guards to reported instances of forced abortions (Holt, 1982; Leonard, 1983) or coerced adoptions (Mann, 1984; Baunach, 1992). Even women returning from sanctioned locales, such as court or visitation, are frequently subjected to vaginal searches for contraband. These searches are humiliating and demeaning. They can also be painful and dangerous, sometimes resulting in bleeding and infection. Access to everyday items like toilet paper and sanitary pads is often highly restricted in women's prisons. Thus, women are dependent on prison staff for even the most basic necessities, which strengthens the oppressive component of the total institution. The older women I interviewed frequently commented on prison rules and regulations, but all of them said they recognized why the rules were in place, and they complied. Misty, a 50-year-old White woman who has been incarcerated for 23 years, stated:

> 'When I first came here there were only 80 inmates and only one building. You could have anything you wanted. Good food like steaks and pork chops. The rules have gotten more petty because of inmates. We create our own madness. You can't smoke in here since last year. Good. I needed to quit anyway.'

Feminist standpoint epistemology posits that experience should be the starting point of knowledge production. More specifically, it insists on the need to view the social world from the perspective of women. According to Millen (1997), this approach draws on Marxist ideas centring the vantage point of the proletariat and suggests that women are an oppressed class with the unique ability to not only understand their own experiences of oppression but to see their oppressors more clearly than can others. That is, the experience of subjugation provides a valid basis for knowledge because it gives access to a closer assessment of the oppressor. Yet women do not have one universal experience of oppression. They have encountered various degrees and forms of discrimination and abuse.

Many of my research participants were survivors of abuse, some nearly fatal. Having survived, they described present healing and plans to 'move on'. Dalia, a 45-year-old Black woman serving a 17½-year prison sentence for trafficking of a controlled substance, reported, "I think it is important to talk to them [other women] about sexual abuse. I was overprotective as a mom, because of what happened to me." Prison provided more than a few with an opportunity to confront issues related to past abuse for the first time.

Survivors of abuse lamented the abusive relationships that were a catalyst to their criminal activity. More generally, they mourned shortfalls in their ability to be a mother to their children or grandmother to their grandchildren. While they recognized their grown children were mature and independent, the women expressed concerns for the well-being of their *grand*children. They wished they could fulfil traditional grandparenting roles and properly bond or see their grandchildren. They considered the job of *raising* their children as finished, so their grandchildren were the new 'little ones' in their lives.

While some of my research participants reported their relationships with adult children to be strong, others viewed their relationships to be severely strained or estranged due to their incarceration. Members of the older incarcerated population recognize that relatives will join their family through birth and marriage and that some will also die during their incarceration. Furthermore, these events will occur without the woman in prison's participation or even occasionally their knowledge.

Contemporary feminist scholars emphasize the importance of women's differences, the power that some women have over others, and the interests that women sometimes share with men. Gender oppression varies in both nature and degree; it is folly and unjust to assume that women identify with each other based on gender alone. Indeed, women are differently positioned within different systems of power (Letherby, 2003). Gender is just one source or mechanism of power and is more or less salient for different people. Age is another mechanism of power; confinement status is another. It is the intent of this study to give voice to the intersection of three such systems of power, namely age, gender, and inmate status, via older incarcerated women – women who have lived through many life experiences and who have stories to tell.

Prison is a sombre environment and the older population endures many years of incarceration full of pains, though some pleasures. Prior research primarily concentrates on negative aspects of incarceration, such as family separation, mental illness, and victimization. The positives, while arguably fewer in number, are largely ignored. Generativity, or giving back to others, offers benefits for both the person who is incarcerated and society, but opportunities to be generative are limited in prison.

The concept of generativity encompasses both desires and behaviours intended to improve the next generation. Generative adults ponder the legacy they will leave behind. In fact, it would seem likely that, due to incarceration, people in prison would not express generativity in the same manner or to the same degree as adults outside of prison. Therefore, it is important to assess if older individuals who are incarcerated have generative desires and, if so, how they can act on them.

The current study explores the experience of incarceration and, most importantly, the presence and execution of generativity among older women. In Erik Erikson's (1950) theory of human development, generativity is a universal stage of life. Thus, adults should experience it whether incarcerated or not. Likewise, ageing and all that it encompasses is inevitable for all adults as well. Yet, it is not clear how older incarcerated people negotiate the prison environment on a daily basis to engage in generative behaviour during their incarceration. Halsey and Harris (2011) have explored this topic to find that a sample of men suggests future generative activities that can even be key for desistance in future criminal activities, while in the confines of prison. But the impact of incarceration on ageing and generativity and vice versa is relatively ambiguous, particularly for women. This book explores a unique aspect in the world of incarceration and one which the majority of us will not experience first-hand, but one that comprises the day-to-day life of the older women of Pewee Valley.

We know that *race* greatly influences day-to-day life for older women in and out of prison. Race shapes the likelihood and hardship of imprisonment *and* experiences of generativity, including expectations thereof. Minorities in the United States and elsewhere are prone to greater criminalization than Whites. They are more likely to be stopped by police, charged with serious offences, detained pre-trial, convicted, and incarcerated than Whites (Kovera, 2019; Nellis 2021; Arnold, Dobbie, and Hull, 2022). In prison, women of colour generally receive harsher treatment than White women. For example, drawing on a large sampling of prison records in the US, Tasca and Turanovic (2018) found that 'Native American, Latina, and Black women had increased odds of placement into administrative segregation relative to their White counterparts' (p 1). As for generativity, it should hold different meanings for those whose cultures centre on the interdependence of extended kin (Stack, 1974), and those who have suffered from stigma and racism (Black and Rubinstein, 2009; Fader, Henson, and Brey, 2022), and those for whom taking care of others has been historically fraught due to racism/sexism. Consider forced wet nursing by enslaved women and, into the present day, employment opportunities narrowed around domestic service. Surely, care is not the same thing as generativity, though they are related concepts;

still, the historical dimensions of one may complicate the other. Evidence suggests that Black women are likely to be more generative than White women (Hart et al, 2001; Newton and Baltys, 2014). A qualitative approach permits a hearing of participants' complex experiences and perspectives. It allows differences to surface, including differences around ageing in prison.

The book is organized as follows. Chapter 2 investigates theory and research on the prison experience for men and women, with a particular focus on the concerns of incarcerated women and how they cope with them. Chapter 3 reviews research on the process of ageing – both in 'free' society and behind bars. In Chapter 4, the concept of generativity is examined more closely. Generative outlets for people who are incarcerated and ways that prisons either impede or allow generativity to occur are discussed along with the methodology of this study. Chapters 5 through 7 reveal findings from interviews concerning parenting and grandparenting getting along in prison as an older person, and generativity. Chapter 8 is a discussion of the findings in general and the contribution of the study in particular. A focus on the unique experiences of being an older, incarcerated woman is explored alongside the concept of generativity.

Notes

[1] Appendix C suggests additional reading on topics adjacent to those covered in this book.
[2] At points, the expression 'free society' is used to denote the world beyond prison. The fact remains that many people in the world, while not in prisons, are not 'free'.
[3] The participants in this study were housed in a correctional institution for women. Gender identity is fluid; having 'female' assigned as one's gender at birth does not mean an individual will retain that identity. However, all of the participants in this study identified as women.

2

Welcome to My Home: Cell Block D

The criminalization of women is by no means a recent phenomenon, but the study of women who are incarcerated as distinct from that of male counterparts is a relatively new development. The prison experience for women is compounded by gender discrimination and expectations. Women in prison have for all practical purposes failed at 'being a woman' as they are unable, due to incarceration, to fulfil their expected roles of wife and mother. Furthermore, they have failed at being a productive member of society; ergo, they are incarcerated and segregated from the morally upstanding members of society. Traditional research on incarceration has effectively devalued the smaller population of women even more, not only by failing to readily appreciate their uniqueness but also by needlessly and routinely comparing them to male counterparts, a group that shares few of the same overall experiences of incarceration. Even now, the literature largely focuses on the negative effects of incarceration, namely the separation of the mother from her children, and remains male-centred as women are still frequently compared to males within the incarcerated population rather than studied on their own merit.

Early research on the prison experience: prisonization and pains of imprisonment

Research has established certain knowledge concerning the experience of incarceration. The dominant theoretical framework for understanding the prison experience stresses prison deprivations and comes primarily from Clemmer and Sykes. Clemmer (1940) defined prisonization as 'the process of assimilation of the prison culture by inmates as they become acquainted with the prison world' (p 299). The effect of the process of prisonization on the person who is incarcerated is to make him or her conform to the norms and expectations of the prison culture. When someone first enters the prison, he or she is stripped of all bases for identity and becomes faceless and anonymous in the new prison environment. The process of prisonization is quicker for some people than for others, and some people may never fully 'assimilate' to prison culture.

When we hear the words 'inmate' or 'prisoner' we often think of men – rightly so, as the vast majority of people in prison are men. Early prison research focused almost exclusively on males and simply ignored the small, but nonetheless important, population of incarcerated women. Clemmer conducted a study of 2,300 males in prison at an undisclosed prison that is reportedly 'typical in respect to discipline, labor, and the various practices found in most other adult correctional institutions' (Clemmer, 1940, p xv). He utilized multiple methodological resources including interviews with people in prison and prison staff, questionnaires, files, essays written by incarcerated people, and standardized tests (for example, the Alpha Army intelligence measure – see Yerkes, 1921). Clemmer identified several conditions – lengthy sentence, unstable personality among free society with a capacity for strong convictions and a particular kind of loyalty, a readiness to integrate into the prison subculture, lack of positive relations with people outside of prison, ready acceptance of the norms of the general penal population, chance placement with other people of a similar orientation, and a readiness to participate in gambling and abnormal sexual behaviour – which he found to increase the effects of prisonization.

While Clemmer (1940) focused on variables influencing the degree of assimilation to the prison setting, Gresham Sykes (1958) studied the characteristics of the prison culture to which the people assimilate. Sykes (1958) reported on his study of the New Jersey State Maximum Security prison in Trenton. In *Society of Captives*, Sykes used a variety of methods including official publications and reports, files, formal interviews, surveys of 200 incarcerated men, participant observation, and informal interviews with people in prison and staff. Order within the prison is described by Sykes as emerging from the set of relationships that one develops to cope with life in captivity, and what he refers to as 'the pains of imprisonment' (Sykes, 1958). The shared sense of suffering and deprivation unifies incarcerated populations to some extent, creating a prison subculture.

Sykes traced the discomforts of the prison experience to five particular 'pains': deprivation of liberty, absence of goods and services, deprivation of heterosexual relations, loss of autonomy, and loss of security. The deprivation of liberty is inherent in the experience of incarceration. The absence of goods and services is painful, whereby the prisoner's basic material needs are met – he does not go hungry, cold, or wet – the person wants not only the necessities of life but also the amenities such as cigarettes, nice clothing, furnishings for their living quarters, and privacy. Sykes referred to the deprivation of heterosexual relations as 'involuntary celibacy' and stated that through imprisonment, the person who is incarcerated is 'figuratively castrated' (p 70). Sykes observed that a male's gendered self, his masculinity, is thrown into question as a result. The loss of autonomy is evident in that the incarcerated person is subjected to a vast body of rules and commands that are designed to control his every behaviour. Sykes quotes one person on the loss of security: 'the worst thing about prison is you have to live with other prisoners' (Sykes, 1958, p 77). People in prison lose the sense of security that they enjoyed in free society because they feel threatened by other prison residents and often fear victimization.

The remainder of Sykes's book investigates adaptation by assuming various 'argot' roles. These are distinctive social roles played by people who are incarcerated in response to the particular problems of incarceration. These 'argot roles' include *rats* (who betray the inmate code of solidarity); *centre men* (who adopt the attitudes and beliefs of prison staff); *gorillas* (who take goods from others); *merchants* (who sell goods to other s); *wolves* (who are aggressive sexual partners); *punks* and *fags* (who are submissive sexual partners); *ball busters* (who give prison staff a hard time); *real men* (who endure prison life with dignity); *toughs* (who are quick to quarrel with all of the others); and *hipsters* (who quarrel only with the weaker people).

In 1962, John Irwin and Donald Cressey departed from Clemmer (1940) and Sykes (1958) by including pre-prison socialization experiences as an important factor in the development of what they determined to be several subcultures within jails and prisons. They did not consider prison subcultures to simply be adjustments to the deprivations of incarceration, but rather aggregates of various criminal and conventional identities with origins outside prison walls. That is, the subcultures are derived from characteristics of people who are incarcerated and experiences prior to incarceration that are imported into the prison institution upon incarceration.

Irwin and Cressey (1962) distinguished people who are incarcerated in terms of three subcultures. *Thieves* are oriented toward the outside criminal world and abide by their own code, not the inmate code. *Convicts* have been raised in the prison system and strictly adhere to the inmate code. *Straights* are not part of the thief or convict subcultures before prison and also reject both of these subcultures while in prison. These broad categories provide a way of examining the influence of latent culture, such as that of thieves and convicts, on prison experiences. In 1970, Irwin, who was once incarcerated himself, presented data supporting this argument.

Irwin (1970) identified three modes of prison adaptation reiterating the subcultures outlined by Irwin and Cressey (1962) and the effect each mode has on both incarceration and post-incarceration experiences. Irwin undertook his research at the California Department of Corrections where he interviewed parolees – 116 men – and parole agents, studied individual files, and attended all parole hearings. Irwin (1970) used the term 'prison career' to describe the process of moving through the stages of imprisonment. In moving through these stages, Irwin identified three adaptive modes. The first mode of adaptation is called 'doing time' and is most common among people who try to maximize their comfort and minimize their discomfort. People who are 'doing time' are usually involved in a number of prosocial activities in prison and often form friendships with other people in prison. The second adaptive mode is 'jailing' and is characteristic of one who cuts himself off from the outside world and strives to establish some level of power within the prison. This type of individual uses friendships and cliques as a means of survival. Finally, 'gleaning' is an adaptation to prison made by those individuals who are looking to better themselves in order to change their lives once released from prison. These people take advantage of educational, vocational training, and treatment programmes within the prison in an effort to improve themselves (Irwin, 1970). Irwin found that 'the convict identity', characterized by strict adherence to the inmate code and orientation to the convicts within the prison, influences the future career of the person who is incarcerated both in prison and after release. That is, they know how to behave in prison prior to incarceration. He found that most convicts are influenced by the convict code and adhere to the major dictum of this code – 'do your own time' – that is, mind your own business.

More recently, convict criminologists have forcefully emphasized the pains of imprisonment by insisting that only convicts know the full horrors of prison life. For example, Ross and Richards (2002) share insights about the corrupt behaviour of correctional officers and random unannounced transfers of people who are incarcerated from one institution to another. Convict criminologists conduct research that illustrates the experiences of 'prisoners' and 'ex-cons', and attempts to combat the misrepresentations of scholars, the media, and government. Like Clemmer, Irwin, and Sykes, most self-identified convict criminologists are men. However, some belated attention is given to the specificity of women's experiences. For example, there is Jean Harris (1988), the notorious former headmistress of The Madeira School for girls in Virginia who made national news in 1980 for the murder of her ex-lover Dr Herman Tarnower. After an argument, Harris shot Tarnower four times at close range. She was arrested and convicted of second-degree murder. Harris offers a woman's perspective on prison life in her 1988 book, *They Always Call Us Ladies*. Harris states, 'It's a fairly normal day here, the usual tragedy all around, some people caring, some people totally unconcerned' (p 25). Her depiction of prison life includes tales of misconduct by correctional officers and first-hand accounts of the emotional anguish suffered by people who lost their children during incarceration. She states, 'One of the many things for which I am grateful is that prison has not extinguished my sense of curiosity. The pleasure of searching, learning, fitting pieces together saves me from many of the horrors that the tedium of prison could reduce me to' (p 19). Harris points to resilience and growth, as the present study does as well.

The early prison studies have afforded a better understanding of how incarceration affects individuals who are confined, and what these individuals do in order to survive their prison term. Later studies would go further in applying concepts such as prisonization, pains of imprisonment, and adaptations thereto, to women. What did they find?

Classic studies of women's survival in prison

Ward and Kassebaum (1965), Giallombardo (1966), and Heffernan (1972) were forerunners in the study of women in prison. The general pattern had been that of ignoring women who are incarcerated s or studying them only for comparison to men, yet these scholars broke new ground as they explored women's prisons exclusively. All three sets of scholars conducted qualitative research and produced book-length works based on their findings. All three entered women's prisons with the ideas of Clemmer and Sykes in mind but arrived at rather different conclusions.

Ward and Kassebaum (1965) executed their study at the California Institution for Women (CIW) in Frontera, where they conducted surveys of 400 people who were incarcerated and 65 prison staff members, interviewed 45 prison residents, and studied files of the people who were incarcerated. Ward and Kassebaum found that the development of identity and prison role adaptation for women are related to the phase of incarceration and their involvement in homosexual relationships. They observed that the process of prisonization causes status degradation and feelings of self-disorientation, apprehension, and a loss of autonomy for women in prison. The social system in prison emphasizes female role expectations which mimic those of free society and homosexual relations in the absence of male partners. Ward and Kassebaum found that identity and loyalty exist in small, intimate pseudo-family groups which often, but do not always, involve homosexual relationships.

Ward and Kassebaum (1965) found that women who were incarcerated suffer from 'affectional starvation', the need for emotional and reciprocal relationships, and that they also possess 'psycho-sexual' needs for interaction with men. They found that a culture had developed at the CIW to meet these needs through emotional and sexual dyads composed of stereotypical female and male roles. Ward and Kassebaum estimated that approximately 50 per cent of the women in CIW had engaged in some form of homosexual activity during their incarceration. They conceptualized homosexuality as a functional adaptation to the deprivations of imprisonment experienced by the women. In the absence of supposedly biological men, the incarcerated women created socially defined men and substituted homosexual relations for heterosexual ones. In addition, Ward and Kassebaum (1965) stated that the phase of a woman's criminal career and prior incarceration experience contribute to her mode of adaptation to prison life. For example, a woman who has an extensive record and previous prison experience enters prison with some level of familiarity and understanding of the prison structure, thereby avoiding the fear and anxiety that are experienced by first-timers.

Giallombardo (1966) interviewed and observed over 100 residents of the West Virginia Women's Federal Reformatory. Her findings replicated those of Ward and Kassebaum regarding homosexual relationships among women. Giallombardo observed, like Ward and Kassebaum, that the informal social order of the prison is based on identities and roles imported from free society. But Giallombardo also observed the adoption of family roles among the women. For example, the traditional feminine roles, such as wife, mother, daughter, or sister, were often paired with masculine roles of stud or butch.

Like Ward and Kassebaum and Giallombardo, Heffernan (1972) examined the assimilation of gender roles from free society into prison life. She utilized surveys, qualitative interviews, personal records, and participant observation at the Women's Reformatory at Occoquan in Virginia. She expanded on the works of Ward and Kassebaum and Giallombardo by examining the relationship between gender roles in free society and the behaviour of people in prison. She found no clear evidence for Sykes's 'argot roles', such as the *right guy* or *merchant*, but she did describe some argot labels which implied a variety of adjustments to prison life for women. Three such roles among women who are incarcerated were the *Square*, the *Cool*, and the *Life*.

According to Heffernan, a woman's initial orientation to prison is typically based on pre-prison experience and identities. She describes three basic reactions. The *Square* is a noncriminal who strives to earn the respect of her fellow women who were incarcerated and officers by focusing on being a 'good Christian woman'. The *Cool* is a sophisticated professional from the underground world of organized crime. She passively manipulates her environment but does not fully commit to prison life because she is only there for a short period. She has prestige, power, and wealth in prison. Finally, the *Life* refers to the recidivist prostitute, shoplifter, and/or drug user/dealer. This group represents over half of the population of women who are incarcerated. Prison life becomes very important to them as they adapt to the traditional inmate code of maintaining loyalty to the inmate society and standing up to prison authorities. Heffernan (1972) stated that 'there is no single inmate adaptive system, but rather that it is composed of multiple subsystems with goals, codes of acceptable behaviour, and means of mutual support that reflect their members' reactions to imprisonment and perceptions of what "the good life" might possibly be in prison' (p 25). Heffernan found that the prison family was a crucial element of the social order of women in prison as it helped them deal with the 'pains' of imprisonment. Women who are involved in pseudo-family groups are, according to Heffernan (1972), the happiest in prison because they are *living* in the prison and thinking little about the outside world.

All three of these studies found some variation among women who are incarcerated, in social life and adaptation behind bars. Homosexual relationships and pseudo-families allow women in prison to fulfil traditional gender roles. Fulfilling psychosocial 'needs', such as doing appropriate gender or being a good mother, can present a challenge to women behind bars. Subsequent critics would reveal that the prominence of homosexual behaviour was grossly overestimated in these early studies of women's prisons. Furthermore, to focus so intently on the women's need to fulfil contemporary social roles behind bars seems simplistic at best. Women must adjust to prison life. Some adjust relatively quickly, perhaps due to having been incarcerated before, but others take more time; still, others never fully acclimate to the prison environment. The grandiose nature of this adjustment consists of all the emotional, physical, and mental pains that the women import into the prison as well as all the pains and deprivations that they endure while in prison. While the early studies of women's prisons identified several creative ways that enable women to satisfy their need to mother (for example, nurture, care, and protect), they represent only the tip of the iceberg to learning about the world of women's imprisonment.

Contemporary ethnographies from a feminist perspective

In the early work of Clemmer and Sykes and even in the early studies of women in prison, the gender-specific hardships of prison life for women received little attention. That is, studies explored modes of adaptation but did not include details about the prison environment to which women had to adapt. In two more recent books, Owen (1998) and Girshick (1999) expose issues that confront women in prison specifically. Feminist theory informs the work of Owen and Girshick. Owen (1998) states that she 'undertook feminist research methods as a way to collect and consider evidence or proof for analytical assertions' (p 23). She sought to document the lives and activities of women in prison and to understand the experiences of incarceration through their own points of view. Girshick (1999) notes that her research 'was undertaken with the explicit objective of examining the gendered nature of women's lives, their options, their crimes, and their time in prison' (p 3). She states that 'a viewpoint grounded in feminism will refuse to accept the male standard as the basis for all of human experience, motivation, or values' (p 25). Feminism also acknowledges patriarchy as a defining force in society.

Barbara Owen (1998) conducted interviews and daily observations in the Central California Women's Facility (CCWF). She interviewed and observed well over 100 people in prison over three years. She asked women to share their own experiences in prison and learned that family separation, sentence length, and degree of allegiance to 'the mix' all have profound effects on how a woman will survive in prison. Across interviews and observations, almost all of the women in her study voiced the extreme importance of children in their lives. The significance of their relationships with their children has an impact on the values shaping prison culture in several ways, such as making conversations about children sacred, acknowledging the intensity and grief attached to these relationships, sanctioning those with histories of hurting children, and other child-specific cultural beliefs or behaviours. Owen also found that family relationships form the foundation for the pseudo-family because they reflect significant roles present in family dynamics in the outside world. She found pseudo-families to be a primary social unit in the organization of the prison culture.

Owen found that sentence length is critical to adjustment and partially determines the ways women organize their time and their commitment to the inmate subculture. Women serving sentences of ten years or more appear to have a common pattern of early difficulties with adjustment (for example, fighting and rebelling against staff), but most women come to accept their sentence and learn to adjust to prison life. Short-termers complain more and may never settle into doing 'clean time' that is, staying out of trouble. Participants in both studies, Owen (1998) and Girshick (1999), talked about the 'convict' or 'inmate code'. Owen found that women do not strictly adhere to the convict code. Long-termers reported diminishing loyalty to the code over the years; claiming the younger people no longer have any respect. Long-termers held a stronger allegiance to the code than younger people who were incarcerated. While there is no uniform interpretation of the 'code', respect toward other people who are incarcerated seems to be central. A respected 'prisoner' does not cause trouble for others. Owen also identifies the 'amorphous concept of "the mix"' (p 179). The mix, as defined by the women in Owen's study, is continuing the behaviour that resulted in the incarceration, such as using or dealing drugs or engaging in prostitution. Most of the women whom Owen interviewed felt that the mix was something to be avoided. Few stated that they were currently in the mix, but many admitted being involved at the beginning of their sentence.

Lori Girshick (1999) conducted interviews with 40 women at a minimum-security prison in North Carolina. She asked them about their lives before and during incarceration. She also interviewed family members, friends, and social service providers in an attempt to clarify the importance of social networks and how they can function or fall apart during the period of incarceration. Separation from family was a major cause of depression, which was the most common mental health problem. Common physical health issues included back problems, headaches, asthma, menstrual problems, arthritis, and ulcers. Girshick reported that the women in her sample felt 'overwhelmingly that the health care at the prison was adequate' (p 99). Girshick reported that participation in pseudo-prison families, initially thought to be extremely prevalent in earlier studies, was low among her sample. Many women viewed prison as a positive experience because it got them off drugs, assisted them in obtaining a GED or job training, or separated them from an abusive partner. She also found that 'for some inmates who are serving very long sentences, these realizations come and go; years of introspection, taking every program available, and fading family contact all have the potential to create frustration' (p 101). Over time, the women she interviewed all felt that they have served their debt to society and are just waiting to be released.

Owen and Girshick identify various and unique difficulties that women face while incarcerated. Indeed, some of the stereotypes that we so readily apply to men in prisons (for example, tattoos and violent temperament) fade away as we recognize that women in prison cannot be depicted in the same terms or images. Now, we can begin to paint the picture of the 'typical' woman who is incarcerated. In doing so, I return to the findings of Owen and Girshick, and the findings of other scholars, in reviewing research on separation from children, drug use, histories of abuse, mental health problems, and physical health. Whereas I review these as distinct concerns, they are anything but. Rather, they intersect in lived reality and have compounding effects on the people who experience them.

Separation from children

I turn to the topic of separation from children with empathy and cautious incredulity for mothers who are incarcerated. While many people would be quick to assume that loss of freedom would be the most difficult element of incarceration, mothers would argue that the loss of their children is worse. Researchers have consistently found that separation from children is the greatest pain of imprisonment for women. This finding holds even for those who may not have been living with their children or those who admit to not being a very good mom prior to their incarceration and those who do not receive frequent contact during incarceration. I say I have cautious incredulity for these women because they generally come to terms with this separation very quickly, and for their own mental survival they live life on the inside by not thinking about life on the outside. Such is a reality of women's prisonization that even now I struggle to comprehend because it does not just affect a few women in prison, but rather the vast majority. Of course, the ability to dismiss this aspect of their lives is a day-to-day struggle and one which affects their experience of incarceration.

According to the Bureau of Justice and Statistics (2000), in 1999, approximately 66 per cent of women in prison were mothers of children under the age of 18, and over 64 per cent were living with their children prior to their incarceration. Sharp and Marcus-Mendoza (2001) found that one in every five incarcerated women in the United States has three or more children. Furthermore, almost all incarcerated women had custody of their children before incarceration, while fewer than half of men did (Church, 1990; Johnston, 1995). Men are less likely than women in prison to even know where their children are living.

Most of the women Owen (1998) spoke with, stressed the paramount importance of children in their lives. She observes that for most women in prison, motherhood is the 'basis for attachment to the outside world not always found among male prisoners' (p 101). Separation from children is often mentally devastating and emotionally agonizing, as women in various studies report that the most punishing aspect of their incarceration is being separated from their children (Van Wormer 1981; Koban, 1983; Baunach, 1985; Clark, 1995).

The emotional strain results in several serious consequences regarding the mental health of incarcerated mothers. Women in prison also experience feelings of guilt because of not being there for their children and worry that the temporary guardians of their children may not adequately supervise them. According to the Bureau of Justice and Statistics (2000), in 1999, more than half of the mothers in state prisons reported that their children were living with a grandparent, while another one fourth reported that their children were living with other relatives. An additional 10 per cent were in foster homes or group homes. Some women may deal with the loss by not allowing themselves to think about their family 'outside'. Some women do not want visits from their children because they do not want them to see their mother in prison. They also fear their own emotional distress of seeing their families but not being able to leave with them. As one participant stated in Owen's (1998) study,

> 'You cannot do your time in here and out on the streets at the same time. That makes you do hard time. You just have to block that out of your mind. You can't think about what is going on out there and try to do your five, ten [or] whatever in here. You will just drive yourself crazy. (p 129)'

One's detachment often undermines the already tenuous relationships with her children, which, in turn, affects her mental health even more (Sharp,

2003). Detachment exacerbates a mother's feelings of guilt and grief over the loss of contact with her children.

Most incarcerated women report that constantly worrying about their dependent children is the most stressful aspect of imprisonment (Bloom and Steinhart, 1993; Farrell, 1998; Owen, 1998). Relatedly, the loss of a relationship with their children is the greatest fear for most incarcerated mothers. Therefore, most women in prison want to take an active role in determining who will take care of their children during their incarceration.

Many mothers in prison are committed to staying involved or becoming involved with their children. Likewise, in Watterson's study (1996) of the experience of incarceration at the California Institute for Women, most incarcerated mothers said that they planned to regain custody upon release. Yet, many mothers in prison have little or no contact with their children. Whereas almost 40 per cent of mothers in prison reported telephone contact at least weekly (Sharp, 2003), the most intimate type of contact, visitation, is generally the most infrequent and logistically problematic. Ekstrand, Burton, and Erdman (1999) found, based on two national surveys conducted by the Bureau of Justice Statistics (see Ekstrand et al, 1999), that over half of the women in state prisons reported never receiving visits from their children. Owen (1998) found that geographical distance and caregivers' reluctance to bring children to the prison were most often cited as reasons why their children never visited them. The physical location of women's prisons is a major inhibitor of visitation. Compared with male prisons, there are fewer correctional facilities for woman who are incarcerated thus, people in prison are commonly housed at a considerable distance, of 100 miles or more, from their families (Bureau of Justice Statistics, 2001). Hence, taking children to visit their mothers is usually costly and time-consuming. Since women in prison and their family members often live in impoverished conditions, the problem of distance can easily translate into no visitation.

Women who are incarcerated, particularly for long periods, face the risk of losing their children, both legally and emotionally (Watterson, 1996). The 1997 Adoption of Safe Families Act allows the automatic termination of custody for incarcerated parents whose children were placed in foster care for 15 or more months. Remarkably, incarcerated women are more likely than incarcerated men to have their parental rights terminated. Children often play a major part in the lives of women. They must navigate life behind bars amid worry about their children on the outside.

Drug use

The reality is that many women who are incarcerated use drugs. A significant number of women in prison report substance abuse and dependency as overwhelming issues. As Henderson (1998, p 579) summarizes her review of research: 'Drug abuse is the primary reason women enter prison and is the primary health problem of women in prison'. According to Chesney-Lind (1997), the War on Drugs has become a war on women: stringent drug laws have greatly contributed to the explosion in women's prison populations. At the time of arrest, women are more likely to test positive for drugs in general and more likely to test positive for cocaine or heroin than their male counterparts (Moon, Thompson, and Bennett, 1993).

Women have a different path to addiction than men, requiring smaller quantities, but frequent drug use results in more health problems among women than men. Women who abuse drugs also report a higher incidence of anxiety, depression, and other psychiatric disorders than men do. Rape and other sexual assault characterize the histories of more substance-abusing women than their male counterparts (Hanke and Faupel, 1993). Women also report having feelings of guilt and shame related to their drug abuse and the impact of their addiction on their families and children. Miller (1990) offers a unique gendered perspective whereby she suggests that female drug abuse is an attempt to control the perceived invasion of physical or psychological boundaries. Miller (1990) states that such invasions range from actual physical episodes, such as rape, battering, and incest, to intrusions of family members who insist that the woman give up her own needs to accommodate theirs. Substance use allows the user to dull the associated pain. Similarly, Reed (1985) observed that women more often report using drugs to cope with life, while men report that they use drugs most often for pleasure or as a social outlet.

For drug users, entry to prison generally means that their use is abruptly discontinued or drastically reduced. Malloch's (2000) study of women who used drugs at five prisons in Scotland and England, revealed that prisons will often provide medication as a short-term detoxification regime or to provide symptomatic relief of withdrawal symptoms. However, the medications provided by prison administrators are minimal compared to the quantities used by the women outside. Consequently, most women who are incarcerated experience the pain of withdrawal symptoms. The extent and nature of these symptoms depend on the drugs and quantity used, length of time the drugs had been used, and individual tolerance levels. Malloch (2000) found that the medication provided by the prisons would sometimes alleviate the most severe aspects of withdrawal, but that the physical and psychological aspects of imprisonment clearly contribute to the distress experienced by many women with drug addictions. For many women, one of the most difficult symptoms of withdrawal is the inability to sleep. Being locked up, usually alone, and experiencing withdrawal with nothing to do but lie awake only worsens the experience. Several women stated that the combination of lack of sleep, feeling sick, uncomfortable physical conditions, and little or no organized activity, left them overwhelmed by their problems. Not surprisingly, incarcerated women in the United States rate drug treatment among the top three types of services to which they would like to have access (Ferraro and Moe, 2003). Since the early 1980s, nearly all US state prisons for women offer some form of drug and alcohol treatment programme. However, studies suggest that there is far more demand for than supply of these treatment programmes. Unfortunately, it is the reasons behind the drug use that must be addressed before any real recovery can take place, and that takes time and resources.

Relational abuse

Scholars have established disproportionately high rates of child sexual abuse and intimate-partner abuse in the histories of women in prisons (Browne, Miller, and Maguin, 1999). According to Human Rights Watch (1996), between 40 to 88 per cent of incarcerated women have been victims of domestic violence and sexual or physical abuse either as children or adults. Baro (1997) studied sexual abuse in a women's prison in Hawaii that housed between 45 to 50 people. She found that between 1982 and 1994, 38 cases of sexual abuse by prison staff were officially acknowledged in Hawaii. Abuse that persists in prison undermines further women's ability to cope with incarceration because of the constant fear of victimization.

Women in prison are far more likely than their male counterparts to be subjected to physical and sexual abuse by prison staff (Amnesty International, 1999). In 1998, male guards outnumbered female guards by almost three to one in women's facilities (Pollock, 1998). Some states have made any form of sexual interaction between staff and residents, whether consensual or not, a felony, but staff/inmate relations continue. A Human Rights Watch study (1996) found that women who reported abuse by prison staff were frequently subject to retaliation by the perpetrator, other guards, or administrators. According to the Department of Justice Office of the Inspector General (OIG) case statistics, most sexual abuse cases for which an investigation is initiated do not result in prosecution (OIG, 2005). The perpetrators are often transferred to other, usually male, prisons. Between 2000 and 2004, the OIG filed 163 sexual abuse cases for prosecution. Of these cases, 73 (45 per cent) were accepted for prosecution. Sixty-five of these cases (40 per cent) resulted in convictions and six of these cases (4 per cent) are still pending prosecution. Eighty-eight cases (54 per cent) were declined for prosecution. Even when prosecuted, the punishments for sexual abuse of people in prison are not very severe. Of the 65 people who were convicted of sexually abusing people who were incarcerated between 2000 and 2004, 48 (73 per cent) received a sentence of probation. Ten of them (15 per cent) were sentenced to less than one year of incarceration (OIG, 2005).

Girshick (1999) examines the retraumatizing effects of prison practices. Women in prison are confronted daily with situations that trigger feelings and memories of previous abuse from childhood and/or adulthood (Girshick, 1999). Pat searches, strip searches, body cavity searches, room searches, and surveillance in shower and toilet areas are commonplace. Those who complain may see disciplinary action or harassment. There is nowhere to hide in prison.

Mental health

Prisons are not able to provide the intensive mental health services that many of those who are incarcerated require. Institutional drug treatment programmes often focus on the addiction rather than the underlying mental health issues that motivate the drug use, issues that the prison situation exacerbates. The abusive and traumatic backgrounds of most incarcerated women typically result in serious depression and even post-traumatic stress disorder. Women who were incarcerated had depression scores more than twice those of the general population samples of women (Ross and Lawrence, 1998). Anxiety is another common mental disorder.

Some speculate that incarcerated women's disproportionately high suicide attempts are a result of women's tendency to internalize anger, while incarcerated men tend to externalize anger by assaulting other people in prison or staff. In one study of incarcerated women, more than one in five reported attempting suicide in the past (Holley and Brewster, 1996). Morris (1987) observed that self-mutilation while in prison, such as cutting, is another way for incarcerated women to manage their feelings. Through self-harm, women can lay claim to their bodies. Women in prison with mental illnesses have problems adjusting to life in prison and are often heavily medicated, which also affects their prison experience by altering their ability to think clearly and perform daily functions such as work detail or interacting with peers and prison staff. Medications often also make people very drowsy causing them to sleep for a large portion of the day.

Health care

Ross and Lawrence (1998) identified certain common medical problems of women in prison including asthma, diabetes, HIV/AIDS, tuberculosis, hypertension, herpes simplex II infection, and chronic pelvic inflammatory disease. Incarcerated women have more serious health problems than women outside of prison because of their increased likelihood of having lived in poverty and experienced limited access to preventive medical care, chemical dependency, poor nutrition, and limited education on health matters (Ross and Fabiano, 1986; Pollock, 1998, 2002; Maeve, 1999).

Prisons are not designed to provide health care specific to women. While most prisons provide very basic health care services, services such as gynaecological and obstetric care are frequently unavailable or inadequate. Annual gynaecological exams are not routinely performed at admission or at any other time during incarceration (Anderson, 2003). One of the major problems in women's prisons is the lack of skilled and available health care. Staff often patronize and minimize prison residents' requests for medical care.

These problems are even greater for pregnant women in prison. Mann (1984) found that prenatal care is often lacking in women's institutions and women have difficulty meeting the nutritional requirements of pregnancy. Furthermore, prisons do a very poor job of providing care in medical emergencies. Yet, Moe and Ferraro (2003) report that women in prison often offer conflicted evaluations of their health care as both poor and inadequate, yet better than could be obtained in the free world. However limited access to health care on the outside, the medical care in women's prisons is also poor in quantity and quality (Pollock, 1998, 2002; Zaitzow and West, 2003). This situation is only expected to get worse as incarceration rates for women continue to increase and as the population of people in prison ages. Chapter 3 considers health challenges for those ageing in prison.

The discussion now turns from problems facing women who are incarcerated to means of coping with such problems. Women in prison must learn to cope with the realities and hardships of incarceration on a daily basis.

Coping among women in prison

Women who are incarcerated share common experiences of abuse, substance use, and motherhood; thus, coping with prison life involves commiserating with others. Males are more likely to adapt to incarceration by isolating themselves, while women seem more likely to adjust by forming close relationships with other people who are incarcerated (Fox, 1975; Maeve, 1999). Women in prison are kinder to each other than their male counterparts. Their friendships with each other are not usually sexual, but rather are based on companionship. Bosworth (2003) viewed homosexual relations in prison as a strategy of resistance to the pains of imprisonment. Furthermore, some research suggests that women's socialization to be caring and to value family relationships has resulted in the structuring of pseudo-families in women's prisons (Giallombardo, 1966; Carter, 1981). Hart (1995) found that women in a high-medium-security prison report higher levels of social support than men. Nonetheless, coping may be challenged when those with whom women are close are transferred, paroled, or die behind bars. Adaptation is an ongoing project.

Prison families provide a supportive network of mothers and fathers, children, sisters, and brothers. Previous researchers referred to these intimate groups as an extended 'family system' or 'kinship system' (Watterson, 1996). In prison families, some women play the parts of men, fathers, husbands, boyfriends, sons, and grandfathers.

Williams and Fish (1974) found that a family unit is an economic unit. People who are incarcerated frequently need commissary products that they have no money to buy and goods and services that cannot be manufactured or stolen without the help of others. The prison family provides the cooperative spirit and organization needed to obtain certain goods and services. Each family member feels a responsibility to help provide economic benefits for the other members of the family. If an incarcerated person who is being punished is deprived of almost all economic goods, other people in the family group are expected to give her extra food, clothing, or information about prison life.

In Watterson's (1996) study of incarcerated women in California, prison families give older women the opportunity to 'mother' younger ones, which helps to fill the void of separation from children and grandchildren. They often give advice and encourage young people to straighten up. Older women who are incarcerated offer experience-based perspectives.

Belknap (2007) reports that some research suggests that pseudo-families were either exaggerated in earlier studies or have become less common in women's prisons than they once were. Fox (1984) found that participation in pseudo-families declined between the 1970s and 1980s. By late 1978, only 27 per cent of women in Bedford Hills, a New York institution for women, reported active membership in a kinship unit; all families had fewer than four members; and involvement in close personal relationships had also declined. In the 1980s, even fewer women reported belonging to such a family system. If they did, their reported loyalty was not as strong as in the past. Indeed, Girshick (1999) found that older people reported younger people in prison to be much less respectful of the 'inmate code', citing instances of 'snitching' and other disloyalties; thus, the prospect of steadfast pseudo-families has diminished.

Incarceration of the 'othered' sex

This chapter provided an overview of the most prominent issues faced by women who are incarcerated, according to research. A process of 'prisonization' occurs for both women and men. Earlier studies regarding women's prisons focused on relationships among people while incarcerated as a method of adaptation while ignoring other important issues such as the exact nuances of the prison environment to which women adapt. In other words, researchers focused on the *how* and did not explore the *what* – tending to assume that the pains of imprisonment were the same for men and women.

One of the overwhelming differences between men and women who are incarcerated is the importance of children in the lives of women. They are far more likely to have been their children's primary caregivers. Yet, visitation is difficult logistically, so many women rarely see their children during their incarceration.

In addition, women import the hardships of life on the outside into the prison. In other words, they are often drug users and victims of abuse. Women also commonly suffer from depression and other mental health issues, as well as suffer from poor physical health while in prison. However, women somehow learn how to successfully negotiate the difficult prison environment. In turn, most people manage to find support from other people in prison with them. People who are incarcerated adapt to their environment by importing many elements of their lives from the free world, such as family roles. Older people often feel pride in the guidance that they are able to give to younger people in prison. While gender offers a unique perspective through which women experience incarceration, the next chapter will add another social dimension: age.

3

Older, Wiser, and Incarcerated

The stereotypical image of a person in prison is a young, healthy man, not an older woman who requires a walker (or Zimmer/walking frame) to navigate the prison grounds. In recent decades, for the first time in American history, we have been faced with the predicament of a steadily increasing ageing prison population. Politicians and correctional systems are confronted with a number of serious issues regarding this unique prison population. The situation of the geriatric person in prison does not enjoy the popularity of other correctional research endeavours such as inmate subculture or educational and vocational programming opportunities. However, the needs of elderly people in prison are a growing concern for prison administrators and researchers as this population continues to grow.

Ageing in general

Only within the past few decades have researchers begun to systematically study the physical health of older people in general (Markides, 1992) and older women in particular. Age is now recognized as having a major impact on health with current research spanning various age groups, including the middle aged and the elderly. In addition to physical health, the process of ageing is also associated with changes in mental health.

Ageing can be defined as the 'sum total of changes occurring in an individual from the time of birth throughout the course of a lifetime' (Mummah and Smith, 1981, p 21). Gerontologists do not agree on a specific chronological baseline for the beginnings of what is commonly called old age. Rather, gerontologists tend to group people into categories. Such categories include 'older' for 55 and older, 'elderly' for 65 and older, and 'aged' for 85 and older (Holzman et al, 1987); or the 'young-old' as 60 to 74, the 'middle-old' as 75 to 84, and the 'old-old' as 85 and over (Yurick et al, 1984).

Ageing is shaped by the interaction of a number of factors including heredity, lifestyle, socioeconomic conditions, and access to medical services.

As people age, physiological changes occur and although changes may vary from one older adult to another, they are referred to as the normal ageing process. The senses dull, and information is processed more slowly and less accurately. Bones are likely to become brittle due to decreased mineral content. Muscle strength weakens and the probability of suffering a debilitating injury from a fall increases (AMA, 1990). The skin becomes dry and wrinkles begin to appear. The decreased functioning of sweat glands and other changes leave the body less able to regulate temperature. Thus, older people are more susceptible to heat and cold. Chronic conditions such as arthritis and diabetes have also been linked to normal ageing. Such diseases may require long-term treatment or management and may result in permanent disabilities.

Ageing is also gendered. Gender differences regarding physical and mental well-being among older adults have been documented (Markides, 1992). Differences in life expectancy and the prevalence of chronic conditions and other health issues among men versus women have been known for some time. Women live longer than men, but they also suffer more from nonfatal disabling conditions, namely arthritis. Degenerative arthritic and rheumatic disorders are the most common chronic illnesses affecting mobility in old age (Ebersole and Hess, 1998). Degenerative disorders of joints and connective tissue affect the entire body. These disorders cause pain, depression, immobility, and disruptions to daily activities. Older women experience more physical symptoms and report higher levels of chronic health conditions than older men (Carmel, 2019).

Chronic conditions range from relatively mild, such as partial hearing loss, to disruptive and disabling, such as arthritis and asthma, to severe and life-threatening, such as diabetes and cancer. One of the most troublesome aspects of many chronic diseases is pain, and pain is one of the most common complaints of elderly adults (Cavanaugh and Blanchard-Fields, 2002). Women also appear to suffer more from minor illnesses and more from limitations in activities of daily living than men. Incontinence troubles some older women, but the embarrassing condition can often be alleviated with proper diet, certain exercises, and medication. Overall, women suffer from a greater incidence of minor physical illness, suffer from more chronic diseases, perceive their health to be poorer, and have a greater prevalence of disability than men. Poor physical health has been linked to poor mental well-being. Gannon (1999) regards physical health as the strongest predictor of the psychological well-being of older women.

While impaired cognitive function is a common complaint among older women, overall gender differences in the prevalence of cognitive dysfunction are relatively minimal (Badgio and Worden, 2007). However, women suffer disproportionately from dementia and chronic fatigue. Depression is also significantly more prevalent among older women than older men, but this is also true earlier in the life course as well. Finally, women experience health issues related to menopause, including an increased risk of osteoporosis and coronary heart disease.

Certain health problems may be compounded for women in prison because they lack the information and resources to cope with or treat their ailments and/or conditions and the prison experience may itself cause health problems. Now, we turn to further examine the phenomena of ageing in prison.

Research specific to ageing in prison

Prior research on ageing in prison has largely focused on men, often centring around issues of respect within the social order. For example, Kreager and colleagues (2017) discussed the power and respect of 'old heads' in male prisons, noting those who are older and/or who have been incarcerated for longer periods of time as a route to status within a prison unit. The productive concept of 'institutional thoughtlessness' has been applied to men (Crawley, 2005). Much less research has been devoted specifically to ageing women in prison. Correctional agencies generally adopt age 50 as the initial age defining older people who are incarcerated (Morton, 1992). Indeed, this population appears 'older', that is, they present problems associated with adults chronologically older than they are due to a number of factors such as socioeconomic status, access to medical care prior to and during incarceration, and the typical lifestyle of most people who are incarcerated (Morton, 1992). Some studies have defined those as young as 40 as 'old' (Aday, 1994). The American Correctional Association (2012) defines the older incarcerated population as those over 55. In a national survey of several state correctional departments, Aday (1999) found that correctional officials generally agree that the typical person who is incarcerated is in their 50s has the physical appearance and common health problems of someone at least ten years older on the outside. However, while many people in prison do exemplify the phrase 'old before their time' others remain in reasonably good health well into their 60s or 70s.

The term 'successful ageing' refers to the phenomenon of adapting and even thriving in one's later years, maintaining a high quality of life (Rowe and Kahn, 1998; Baltes and Mayer, 1999; Crosnoe and Elder, 2002). It is not generally treated as a gendered issue. Older women are still largely either ignored in regard to the idea of ageing well or are considered only in comparison to older men. Some of the indicators of a good quality of life are health, absence of cognitive/psychological distress, and availability of supportive family and friends (Haug and Folmar, 1986).

What follows is a review of previous research on ageing in prison regarding three main areas: physical health, mental well-being, and relationships with family and friends. As scholarly focus on older women who are incarcerated is relatively new, research on this particular subpopulation is limited. Thus, my review includes both the more numerous studies regarding males as well as the handful of studies focusing only on older women in prison.

Physical health

Health problems are common among older people who are incarcerated as they often have weakened immune systems and increased susceptibility to disease caused by the compounding effects of multiple health conditions such as diabetes and high blood pressure. Chronic medical illness and/or a history of drug and/or alcohol use also play an important role in the prevalence of infectious diseases in this age group. The elderly are particularly susceptible to the various diseases that spread within institutions. Airborne viruses such as influenza and respiratory viruses are common among older people who are incarcerated.[1] Falter (1999) found gastrointestinal infections to be common as well. Older people are more susceptible to urinary tract infections. Hepatitis and pneumonia can also quickly affect elderly people who are confined. Consequently, many older people in prison require various daily medications. Douglass (1991) conducted in-depth interviews with 79 males who were incarcerated aged 60 and older and housed in 13 correctional facilities in Michigan. He found that out of the 79, 31.6 per cent were taking over-the-counter pain medications, 36.7 per cent were taking prescription medications for pain, 37.9 per cent were taking high-blood pressure medications, and 24.1 per cent were taking nitro tablets for chest pain.

Studies of older people in prison have mostly sampled males. These studies suggest the health challenges of ageing behind bars. Douglass (1991) found that only 5 per cent of his sample of 79 men who were incarcerated rated their health as excellent, 78 per cent rated their health as fair or good, with the rest rating their health as poor. When they compared their physical health conditions to what they were two years prior, 24 per cent indicated their health was worse, 58 per cent said it was the same, and 18 per cent said it was better. Similarly, Colsher, Wallace, Loeffelholz, and Sales (1992) studied the health of 119 incarcerated males aged 50 and older in seven Iowa state correctional facilities. Most (65 per cent) rated their health as excellent or good, but almost half reported that their health had worsened since incarceration. The men reported a high incidence of chronic illness and some limitations in physical functional ability. The illnesses reported by the participants included arthritis (45 per cent), hypertension (39 per cent), ulcers (21 per cent), prostate problems (20 per cent), myocardial infarction (19 per cent), emphysema (18 per cent), and diabetes (11 per cent). Age was also significantly correlated with chronic illness. Those 60 years and older, in Colsher et al's study, reported higher rates of chronic illnesses than those between 50 and 59 years of age.

Aday (1995) surveyed 102 older incarcerated men aged 50 and over in Mississippi. Most participants in his sample (75 per cent) were able to perform routine self-care activities and engage in some prison activities. Hypertension, arthritis, and heart problems were the most common conditions reported by the incarcerated population over the age of 50. Twenty-seven per cent of Aday's (1995) respondents felt that their health was excellent or good, 28 per cent reported that their health was only fair, while 45 per cent reported their health as poor compared with their perception of the health status of their peers. In comparison to their health two years ago, only 8 per cent of those surveyed felt it was better, 57 per cent reported that it was about the same, and 32 per cent felt that it was worse. Furthermore, only 11 per cent expected their overall health to improve over the next two years, 28 per cent expected no change, and 61 per cent expected that their health would worsen over the next two years.

Most prisons are dealing with an ageing prison population; thus, the health problems of older residents are a phenomenon that is shared across all states. In 2001, Aday (2001), with the help of personnel from the Tennessee Health Department, conducted a survey of 318 people who were incarcerated, 302 men and 16 women who were 60 years of age and over in correctional facilities in Tennessee. This study was intended to provide a comprehensive health assessment for those in this age group. Hypertension was the most frequently reported health condition, followed by arthritis, heart disease, pulmonary disease, diabetes, and emphysema. Although most of the sample was functionally independent, 20 per cent of them required a walking stick or cane, walker or Zimmer frame, crutches, or wheelchair for mobility.

Research on women who are incarcerated yields similar findings. Women in prison are roughly seven to ten years 'older' than their chronological counterparts in the free community and they often feel that way (Reviere and Young, 2004). Kratcoski and Babb (1990) sampled both men and women in prison over the age of 50 from eight federal prisons and seven state prisons in Pennsylvania, Florida, and Ohio. They found that 47 per cent of the older women claimed that their health was poor or terrible compared with 25 per cent of the men, a statistically significant difference. Chronic health problems were both physical and psychological. Substance abuse, overeating, worry, depression, heart, respiratory, and degenerative illnesses were common.

Genders and Player (1990) provide an in-depth account of the experience of ageing in prison in their study of 25 women lifers in a British prison. They found that lifers experience an overwhelming fear of deterioration in their physical health and psychological well-being. The women commonly suffered from skin and weight problems that were attributed to a lack of fresh air and a poor diet. Indeed, poor diet is reflected in the finding that women offenders serving sentences in excess of 18 months typically reported gaining an average of 20 pounds over a three-year period (Genders and Player, 1990).

Aday and Nation (2001) interviewed 29 older women aged 50 or older at Tennessee's Prison for Women. They found that 20 per cent of these women considered their health to be poor and another 51 per cent reported their health as only fair. The women reported chronic health problems such as hypertension, arthritis, and some type of heart condition. Depression was also very prevalent. One third of the sample felt that their health would worsen over the next year. Over half said that they currently smoked and about 25 per cent reported having had a previous drug or alcohol problem in the past that was exacerbating their current health status. They also found that poor health caused mobility problems as older people in prison may not be able to walk long distances or stand for long periods of time.

Older people require more health care than younger people, and women require more health care than men. Therefore, older women who are incarcerated will likely need more medical services than any others. Diabetes, hypertension, menopause, arthritis, and cancers of all types, especially lung, breast, and cervical, are of concern to older women in prison (Caldwell, Jarvis, and Rosefield, 2001). Furthermore, hysterectomies can cause dramatic physical and mental problems with which women must cope. Young (1998) assessed the health of 129 women residents at a Washington state prison. She found that 53.5 per cent of the women were on medication when they entered prison and about 73 per cent of them smoked, which is almost three times more than women do in free society. More than 60 per cent of the sample reported at least one major medical problem. They also received a number of services outside the prison such as chemotherapy, radiation, or dialysis.

Mental well-being

Mental health also affects an incarcerated person's ability to function successfully in the prison environment. Approximately 300,000 incarcerated individuals in state and federal prison facilities either have been found to suffer from a current mental condition or have stayed overnight in a mental hospital, medical unit, or treatment facility (Ditton, 1999). Vitucci (1999) further estimated that about 210,000 of those 300,000 people have severe mental illnesses. Therefore, approximately 15 per cent of state and federal people who are incarcerated are mentally ill. While dementia becomes more prevalent during old age, the prevalence of substance abuse problems, anxiety disorders, and schizophrenia also significantly increase during middle age.

In a national survey of people under correctional supervision, Ditton (1999) found that people between the ages of 45 and 54 were the most likely age group to be classified as mentally ill. Approximately 20 per cent of those incarcerated in state facilities, 10 per cent of those in federal facilities, and 23 per cent of those in jail in this age range reported at least one mental illness. Incarcerated people aged 55 and older also reported symptoms of mental illness. Approximately 15 per cent of state, 9 per cent of federal, and 20 per cent of jail residents in the 55 and above age group were identified as mentally ill.

Koenig and colleagues (1995) found that depression, anxiety, and psychiatric disorders were much more common in a group of 95 people who were incarcerated over the age of 50 than among men in a matched sample in free society. Overall, 54 per cent of these older people fit the criteria for having an active psychiatric disorder. Those with a previous history of alcohol or drug abuse were particularly at high risk of having a current psychiatric disorder. Booth (1989) contends that older people who are incarcerated have more stressors to contend with than younger individuals who have not experienced poor health or major changes in vitality and endurance. The noisy, physically strenuous prison environment also creates a stressful situation.

The prison environment inevitably causes stress, particularly for older residents. Prisons are typically designed for young, physically active people. They often consist of campus-style housing with living units and support services located in various buildings spread out over wide areas. This design often requires one to walk long distances to obtain meals, medical services, and other necessities. Stairs, weather conditions, and structural difficulties, such as long distances between buildings, cause additional problems for older people with physical and mental disabilities (Newman, Newman, and Gewirtz, 1984). Aday and Nation (2001) found that very few of the older women they interviewed at Tennessee's Prison for Women were satisfied with their living conditions. Older, frail participants found stale air from smokers, top bunking, and being housed too far away from the dining room and bathrooms to be significant environmental problems. While they found that 96 per cent of the 29 participants could walk independently, well over half reported difficulty walking long distances or standing in line for longer than 15 minutes, both of which they are sometimes required to do. Older women housed in the general prison population expressed a need for greater privacy. Aday and Nation (2001) found that three fourths of the women in their sample found the current housing situation to be crowded, unpleasant, and very noisy. The older people found younger people to be noisy and inconsiderate. Similar studies have found that both men and women who are incarcerated prefer to live with people of their own age (Walsh, 1989).

Walsh (1990) introduced the importance of structure for older people in prison. Older people prefer stability and predictability more than younger individuals do. Prisons provided structure with guidelines for action, penalties for noncompliance, and rewards for compliance. Older people also prefer stability. According to Walsh (1990), older individuals are willing to accept some boredom in return for dependency and consistency. As time passes, the older person's need for structure increases. As older people serve their time, they become more attached to the defined prison environment. They become especially concerned to maintain predictable prison routines. As ageing brings personal losses, such as the decline of personal health and the death of loved ones, control over the immediate prison environment becomes more important.

Bachand (1984) found the health of elderly people in prison to be compounded by excessive mental worry. McCarthy (1983) classified approximately half of a sample of 248 older incarcerated people as 'worriers'. They were worried about their health, family members, and their safety. Genders and Player (1990) found woman lifers also expressed fears of physiological deterioration that were linked to their low sense of self-esteem, dread of institutionalization, loss of self-concept, and inability to conceive of a future. The fear associated with being reduced to a passive mental state is a significant stressor for many women serving life sentences. However, the most common source of worry and difficulty in adjustment stems from separation from family members.

Relationships with family and friends

Studies have linked social support with positive health outcomes for seniors in free society (Thoits, 1995; House, Umberson, and Landis 1988). Social support refers to assistance provided to individuals (emotional or tangible), the frequency of contact with others, and the perceived adequacy of that support (Hooyman and Kiyak, 2002). In free society, older adults often relocate to be nearer to their families. Research consistently shows that living near children facilitates the existence of support services (Silverstein and Litwak, 1993). Further, support for socioemotional selectivity theory suggests that as individuals in free society age, interaction and perceived closeness with family members increase (alongside a decrease in interaction with friends and acquaintances) (Carstensen, 1992). US prisons, particularly women's prisons, are frequently located in rural areas, whereas most of the residents' families live in urban areas, which results in isolation from family. In many states, there is only one facility for women and travel may be too expensive and inconvenient to allow for frequent visitation from family and friends.

The loss of contact with family and friends on the outside is a major concern for any individual who is incarcerated. The length of incarceration, coupled with growing older may serve to decrease the number of family and friends on the outside. Most recognize that the prospects for maintaining relationships over a long time are slim and they are often forced to construct a new sense of their social reality so that life can proceed. Santos (1995) observed that changes in families, such as marriages, births, and deaths, will occur without the participation of the incarcerated individual and, sometimes, knowledge. The desertion of family and friends is hard for people serving time in prison to accept.

Wikberg and Foster (1989) interviewed 31 long-term residents at Angola Prison, a men's prison in Louisiana. They found that most have had few visitors over the years. Their parents have died, their brothers and sisters are older and have stopped visiting and, if they were married, their wives have divorced them. A survey done by Sabath and Cowles (1988) determined that family contacts, education, and health had the greatest effects on positive institutional adjustment. Older men who were able to maintain regular family contacts were better adjusted than those who could not. However, women enjoy greater longevity than men, and they are also more likely to live alone and outlive social support systems (Morton, 1992). Older people doing time often lose touch with the outside world and outlive many relatives and friends. The lack of a supportive social network can be devastating, as social support from family and friends is one of the main buffers against the effects of stress during incarceration.

In Aday's (1995) study of incarcerated men in Mississippi, an estimated one third of the sample was married. Seventy per cent reported that their parents were deceased, over two thirds had living siblings, 72 per cent had living children, and 53 per cent had living grandchildren. Twenty-four per cent of the sample reported 'often' or 'fairly often' receiving visits from their family, but 38 per cent stated that they had contact with family members through telephone calls and letters sent and received (Aday, 1995). Forty-one per cent of the sample claimed to 'never' have been visited by family. Visits from friends were less likely overall. Imprisonment disrupts family relationships, family roles, and life in general. The longer the normal roles of parent, child, or grandparent are disrupted, the more difficult it is to re-establish those roles.

In Kratcoski and Babb's (1990) study of male and female people who were incarcerated they found more than 50 per cent of the older women in their sample reported never having visitors, compared with 25 per cent of the older men. One explanation they offer is the lesser proportion of married men and women who were incarcerated. However, in their study at Tennessee's Prison for Women, Aday and Nation (2001) found that some older incarcerated women prefer not to have frequent visits and prefer to rely more on letters and phone calls to stay in touch with family. In their study, 27 per cent reported that they had living parents, 86 per cent had children, and 65 per cent had grandchildren. Nearly all (93 per cent) said that they remained in contact with their family. Only 10 per cent of them receive weekly visits, but 70 per cent reported that they talked to family members each week on the phone. Almost all of them reported that they had family and friends on the outside whom they could depend on for support. Aday (2003) notes that for some older people who are incarcerated and serving longer sentences, visits from family on the outside can be painful and can cause a grief reaction. The inability to fulfil the role of parent or grandparent every day can be frustrating. Therefore, it becomes easier for people to do their time by maintaining a degree of social distance from their families and free society. Aday and Nation (2001) posit that seeking comfort among an inner circle of friends who are also incarcerated for social support is one way some older women cope with long-term incarceration and family separation.

Wrinkles, prison stripes, and everything's not alright

Ageing is an inexorable process. Prison does not shield older people from the realities or complications associated with old age. If anything, incarceration along with previous lifestyle hastens poor health and mental illness. Mental health is also a concern among older people in prison because they suffer from more mental illnesses than younger people, including dementia and depression. It is important to explore the impacts of incarceration during middle to late adulthood. While policy makers are well aware of the ageing prison population, little has been done to systematically identify and manage the various needs of older people. Like older men, older women in prison may be in prison for the first time late in life or may be growing old in prison as a result of long sentences. Incarcerated women are still underrepresented in the current research literature; studies focusing on older women in prison are even rarer. Women who are incarcerated have more chronic conditions and seek more medical attention than men in prison. Very little is known about the negative and positive experiences of older women behind bars. Further research is necessary to understand the needs of older women serving time, which also may include the need to contribute to the well-being of others. The next chapter orients to the positive, exploring the phenomenon known as generativity.

Note
[1] The COVID-19 pandemic brought new hardships for the prison population in general and its ageing subpopulation in particular (Prost et al, 2021).

4

A Positively Negative Experience

This chapter explores the notion of generativity, or a desire to give to others and a concern for the next generation, with attention paid to generativity as a feature of the life course. Life course sociologists explore the stages people go through during a lifetime, often with an eye toward what society expects of individuals at certain life stages and how these expectations are stratified (Gilleard and Higgs, 2016). Generativity has been conceptualized in different ways by various scholars but with the consensus that it is a stage of life first experienced during middle adulthood. Therefore, middle-aged people in prison should also experience this stage but face institutional barriers to being generative. That is, the authoritative nature of the prison institution limits the ability of people who are separated from free society to 'give back'.

Generativity is the 'concern in establishing and guiding the next generation' (Erikson, 1950, p 267). Through generativity, adults seek to care for and contribute in positive ways to the world and the people they leave behind. People hope the lives of their children and the children of others will be good and will have meaning and value. Erikson (1950) regarded generativity as the psychological focus of the seventh stage in his eight-stage model of human development.

According to de St. Aubin and his colleagues (2004), generative adults hope to pass on the most valued traditions of the culture, teach the most valued skills and outlooks, impart wisdom, and foster the realization of human potential in future generations. Whereas Erik Erikson first coined the term 'generativity' and explored its implications and influence on adult development in his 1950 work *Childhood and Society*, it was his concept of identity that caught immediate attention and made Erikson famous. As McAdams and Logan (2004) observe, it was not until the 1980s that generativity finally emerged as a topic for empirical research among life span developmental psychologists, personality psychologists, and sociologists.

Erik Erikson's eight life stages

Whereas Freud stated that personality was developed and permanently defined during childhood, Erikson (1950) believed that personality continued to develop during adulthood in a series of eight stages that extend from birth to death. All of the stages in Erikson's theory are present at birth, but the resolution of each stage is determined by the interaction of the body, mind, and cultural influences at various points throughout the life course. More specifically, each stage is characterized by a psychosocial crisis, which is based on both physiological development and the demands put upon the individual by parents and other social actors and forces. Erikson (1950) presents 'a system of stages dependent on each other' (p 272). Each of these stages builds on the preceding stages while paving the way for subsequent stages.

Erikson divided his eight life stages into the experiences of children, young adults, middle-aged adults, and older adults. Corresponding to these stages is a set of ego qualities that emerge from critical periods of development (Erikson, 1950). Middle adulthood, which is the focus of the current study, is marked by the seventh stage of generativity versus stagnation.

Erikson referred to the successful outcome of each stage as 'the virtue'. Each of the life stages is associated with a specific 'virtue' that signifies a healthy ego and the existence of personal strength. Erikson defined virtue as that which reflects the inner quality and eventually the integration of one's complete character (Erikson, 1950). The virtue of the generativity stage is care.

Erikson believed that once the adult has gained a sense of self in stage 5 and established long-term bonds of intimacy through marriage or friendships in stage 6, then she or he is psychosocially ready to commit to the larger society and its continuation and/or improvement through the next generation.

Erikson presented the bearing and raising of children as key tasks in becoming a generative adult. Parents are actively involved in providing for the next generation as embodied in their own offspring. However, Erikson was careful to point out that the mere fact of having and raising children does not lead one to achieve generativity (Erikson, 1950). Further, any adult, even one who does not rear children, is capable of contributing to the next generation. Erikson would later state even more explicitly that generativity is not limited to parenthood (Erikson, 1963). In *Gandhi's Truth* (1969) Erikson found in the life of Gandhi a generativity extended to the care of an entire nation. Nevertheless, Erikson believed that the parent is the essential agent for ensuring physical certainty for the continuity of the species and the mental health of the young generation. Parenthood challenges the adult to believe in the future of the species and to foster this belief in their children.

Erikson's life stage model and subsequent works that utilized his model have been criticized for reflecting the male experience and a male perspective on development. Rosalind Barnett and Grace Baruch (1978) argued that women's varying roles do not correlate with chronological age the same as those of men. Patterns of timing and commitment are unique, thus, creating numerous combinations of career, marriage, and children. Carol Gilligan (1982) proposed that as a result of early object relations, women place greater importance on attachments, intimacy, and relationships, while men place greater importance on separation, individualism, and autonomy. Carol Ryff and Susan Migdal (1984) observed that, for the most part, these criticisms have been raised primarily on the conceptual or theoretical level and there have been few empirical studies to test whether Erikson's model actually is or is not relevant for women.

Ryff and Migdal (1984) surveyed 100 women, 50 women aged 18 to 30, and 50 women aged 40 to 55, on issues of intimacy and generativity. They found that the literature's emphasis on generativity as a preoccupation of later years was supported for middle-aged women who perceived themselves to be more generative than they were as younger adults. Young women, on the other hand, rated themselves as more generative than they anticipated themselves to be in middle age. Ryff and Migdal question the relevance of Erikson's model for women's development, as women younger than age 40 reported thoughts of generativity, a stage Erikson posited as coinciding with middle age. Nonetheless, generativity continues to be regarded as a universal life stage of adulthood.

Expanding on generativity

Erikson introduced the concept of generativity more than 50 years ago. Since that time, research and theorizing on generativity have slowly gained in popularity. Several researchers have made theoretical statements about generativity that appear to expand on and depart from certain Eriksonian ideas (Browning, 1975; Kotre, 1984; McAdams, 1985), several of which will be discussed more thoroughly under appropriate subheadings later in this chapter. For the purposes of this project, I believe it is important to dissect the concept of generativity. Incarcerated women face many challenges, survival, arguably, being the most fundamental. However, it is important that their means of generativity are not lost in translation or otherwise overlooked due to the potential perception of them as trivial by comparison to generative adults in free society. It has already been established that generativity is an issue for adults, not for children (Erikson, 1950). Furthermore, generativity is likely to occur around middle age for most adults. While Erikson emphasized the importance of parenthood, generativity is arguably achievable with or without bearing children. Generativity is about the next generation, both one's own children and those of others. Indeed, Erikson (1950) stated that not all parents are generative and that generativity is not limited to parenthood. It is about being a responsible citizen, a contributing member of a community, and a leader. Generativity involves the creation of a product or legacy in one's own image (McAdams, 1985). It involves behaviour that includes the conservation, restoration, preservation, nurturance, and/or maintenance of that which is deemed worthy of such behaviour, such as nurturing children, preserving good traditions, protecting the environment and participating in rituals (in school, church, or home) that connect generations and ensure continuity over a period of time (McAdams, Hart, and Maruna, 1998). Since generativity is about so many things, one can seemingly be very creative in achieving it.

A model of generativity

McAdams and de St. Aubin (1992) recognized that, notwithstanding various research efforts on the concept of generativity (Erikson, 1950; Ryff and Migdal, 1984), there had yet to be any systematic theory of generativity. For example, Erikson (1950) did not theorize about generativity as an evolving process, as he only regarded it as an anticipated stage in the adult life course. In other words, Erikson did not provide a comprehensive theory of generativity that included specific thoughts of motivations and development. McAdams and de St. Aubin (1992) identified seven features of generativity. These features centred on both the individual's and society's goal of providing for the next generation. The first two features, *cultural demand* and *inner desire*, are viewed as the ultimate motivational sources for generativity, and they come together in the third feature, *conscious concern*. When conscious concern is supported by the fourth feature of *belief* in the goodness of the human species, it may stimulate the fifth stage of *generative commitment*. The final two features are *generative action* and *narrative*. I will now explore each feature in greater detail.

McAdams and his colleagues (1998) state that generativity stimulates inner desires that feel natural because caring for the next generation has been a consistent part of human evolution. Generativity that goes beyond bearing and raising one's children may simply be an expansion or generalization of instinctive patterns associated with reproduction and care of offspring. In other words, there is an instinctive desire to be generative. However, according to McAdams and de St. Aubin (1992), there is also external cultural demand. Culture strongly influences the form and the timing of generative expression. Indeed, all societies require, to some extent, that adults care and provide for the next generation. The very continuity of a society's traditions, values, and practices depends on adults transmitting those cultural elements to future generations. McAdams, Hart, and Maruna (1998) maintain that generativity is wedded to the cultural setting. The generative adult must work within the economic and ideological frameworks of society if she or he is to assume a generative role as a teacher, mentor, advocate, leader, activist, and citizen. The generative adult who rejects the dominant values and norms of a society or experiences challenging or restrictive conditions will find an alternative framework within which to express generativity (McAdams, Hart, and Maruna, 1998).

Concern for the next generation refers to an overall attitude regarding generativity in one's life and social world. It is anticipated that the level of concern varies among individuals. Some adults may have an intense concern for and interest in promoting the next generation, while other adults may express little to no concern and interest. McAdams and Azarow (1996) found that generative concern was significantly associated with self-reports of life satisfaction, happiness, self-esteem, goal stability, and sense of coherence in life, and was negatively associated with depression.

McAdams, Hart, and Maruna (1998) agree with Erikson that generative commitment and generative action are supported by what he called a belief in the human species. The life stories of highly generative adults suggest a deep and constant faith in the fundamental goodness of humanity. Notwithstanding harm-doing, people can redeem themselves. Adults who focus on generativity in their life narratives build identities on a foundation of faith in humankind. They affirm their hope for the future and support their convictions that their own lives have ultimate meaning and significance by way of their connection to the next generation. In effect, their stories actualize those premises and, from a narrative criminological perspective, the stories themselves actualize good in the world (Presser, 2009).

McAdams and de St. Aubin (1992) likewise consider generativity to be a storytelling project. They state that beginning in late adolescence and young adulthood, men and women attempt to construct more or less integrative narratives of the self to give their lives unity and purpose. Furthermore, they observe that it is not uncommon for adults to leave considerable space in their life stories for generativity as it is an important theme in life stories of midlife adults. Generative narration refers to the characteristic way in which individuals make sense of their generative efforts: they put these efforts in the context of a life story (McAdams, Hart, and Maruna, 1998). However, adults show significant individual differences with respect to generative narration.

Generativity and imprisonment

The model of generativity assumes that an individual lives in free society and is exposed to the pressures and expectations associated with it. It also assumes that individuals want to care for future generations because they were cared for by others (McAdams, 1985). The model emphasizes hope for the future and faith in the basic good in humanity. However, people in jail or prison have been removed from free society to live under very unique and restricted circumstances. Incarcerated women, in particular, commonly report having suffered abuse at the hands of those who were supposed to care for them. Women in prison are often a 'forgotten' population which leaves little room for hope or belief in human goodness. The problems of generativity among people who are or have been incarcerated have not gone unexamined. In fact, several studies have explored the nature of and opportunities for generative behaviour during and after incarceration.

Maruna (2001) found that generativity is a central theme in the narrative accounts provided by men and women who have 'gone straight' after a life of crime. Maruna (2001) analysed 20 published autobiographies written by successfully and unsuccessfully reformed ex-convicts in terms of theme, plot structure, and character. He found a prototypical reform story, among the successful ex-convicts, featuring generativity. He found that the self-narratives of ex-convicts who were successful in desisting were significantly more care-oriented, other-centred, and focused on promoting the next generation. He also identified, among these desisters, a life plan intended to 'give something back' and help others in similar circumstances. One participant described a desire to 'give people my life – you know, experiences – what I been through' (Maruna, 2001 p 103). Another participant said, 'Hopefully, I'll be something to other people' (Maruna, 2001 p 105). In fact, many of the participants suggested that they were publishing their stories so that younger generations could learn to avoid making the same mistakes that they did. Maruna (2001) argues that the sense of higher moral purpose that accompanies generative commitments might be necessary for resisting criminal activities. Criminal behaviours provide individuals with at least momentary escapes into excitement, power, and notoriety (Maruna, LeBel, and Lanier, 2003). If 'going straight' means accepting docility and stigma, there is little reason to resist criminality. Maruna (2001) found that the intrinsic rewards and social respectability of generative roles provide an appealing alternative to both these subjugated outcomes and criminal behaviour. White (2000) found that ex-convicts based their self-conceptions on identities as 'wounded healers'. That is, they have tried to find some meaning in their shame-filled life by turning their experiences into warnings or hopeful stories of redemption for younger people in similar situations.

Given such findings, it seems reasonable that the correctional system would seek out every opportunity to support and even hasten the development of these desires among those who are incarcerated. Erikson (1950) stated that the opposite of generativity is stagnation, and Maruna and his colleagues

(2004) observe that there is no better word for describing contemporary prison life where almost everything about the process seems designed to prevent natural maturational processes among prison residents.

The structure and rules of prisons create barriers to those trying to lend support to their families or to achieve other personal goals. People working for a dollar a day are not able to make financial contributions to their families. In fact, these people often become financial burdens to their family members (Maruna, LeBel, and Lanier, 2004). People in prison often require money in order to buy necessities from the commissary. Parenting behind bars is difficult and generally emotionally painful. People in prison frequently develop a sense of being doomed to a life of addiction, criminality, and prison, which is similar to the pessimism with which society seems to view their potential to reform. Maruna, LeBel, and Lanier (2004) observe that the current correctional system mainly lacks opportunities for the promotion of generative ideals and behaviours, but a few potentially generative projects and activities can be found. What follows are three areas of generative potential within the prison system as identified by Maruna and his colleagues (2004).

Community service

Some programmes promoting generative opportunities can be found in prisons. Community service is one. Yet, despite its origins as a rehabilitative endeavour, community service is no longer used as a strength-building exercise but is generally manual, menial, and arduous (Caddick, 1994). Community service opportunities in prison are rare, particularly for women. According to a strengths-based framework, community service work would be voluntarily agreed upon and would involve challenging tasks that utilize the talents of the individuals who are in prison in useful roles in the community (Dickey and Smith, 1998). For example, in a partnership programme with Habitat for Humanity, residents from 75 prisons, along with community volunteers, built over 250 homes for low-income families in 1999 in Illinois, Michigan, Texas, and Wisconsin (Ta, 2000). Furthermore, teams of people who are incarcerated have voluntarily helped in fighting the forest fires ravaging national parks in the western region of the United States. In the year 2000, one in six of the crewmembers fighting fires was incarcerated (Jehl, 2000). Jehl (2000) interviewed participants in this programme and found that such participation made them proud and promoted a positive self-image. One participant stated, 'Being in this program makes all the difference. ... Now I can tell my four-year-old son that his dad isn't in prison, he's out fighting fires' (Jehl, 2000, p A1). Another firefighter who was incarcerated stated, 'Most of my life, I took things from people, and now it's time to give something back' (Jehl, 2000, p A1). The community effort gave people who were incarcerated a sense of confidence and contribution that they would normally not receive behind bars.

People incarcerated in many states are involved in providing respite care to fellow prison residents dying of AIDS and other illnesses in the prison facility. There are often long waiting lists of people who are incarcerated seeking to volunteer to be caregivers (Stolberg, 2001). A warden at one prison with a hospice hypothesized that its nurturing climate helps the patients first, then the volunteers, and finally the whole prison. These hospices have been found to have unforeseen effects such as decreases in prison violence (Kolker, 2000).

'Professional ex'

Generative activities have long been the focus of programmes such as Alcoholics Anonymous (AA) and Narcotics Anonymous (NA). These programmes allow for the transformation of identity from victim to survivor to helper. Members who stay connected to the programme, deemed as 'wounded healers' (White, 2000), eventually take on the role of sponsors and mentors to the next generation of recovering addicts. Brown (1991) uses the term 'professional ex' to refer to a person who desists from a deviant career by replacing it with an occupation as a paraprofessional, lay therapist, drug counsellor, or training officer. He estimated that approximately three quarters of the counsellors working in the over 10,000 substance abuse treatment centres in the United States are former substance abusers themselves. This type of role modelling occurs in prisons as well. People in prison frequently form informal mentoring systems in which older people become parent figures to newer, younger people in prison. Based on his own experience in prison, Irwin (1980) emphasizes that self-help groups 'open doors ... to a variety of conventional endeavors' (p 94). Hamm (1997) observed that more people who are incarcerated belong to self-help groups than to any other form of prison programme. Members of these groups try to see themselves as kind and capable individuals who are able to lead fulfilling lives despite their current condition of incarceration.

In a recent trend referred to as the 'New Recovery Movement' (White, 2000), wounded healers are asked to become recovery activists. That is, they are asked to take a proactive role in mentoring others and encouraging them to change. These and other efforts offer individuals the opportunity to share their experiences and to help others. They willingly give their time in the service of helping others who are not as far along in the rehabilitation process, in a sense, the next generation of wounded healers.

Parenting from prison

Parenting from prison is made very difficult due to the logistical and emotional issues involved in bringing children to prisons for visits. Most families must travel long distances. Even telephone calls are costly. While research has found that the children of incarcerated parents often become confused, unhappy, and socially labelled, less is known about the impact of prison on a person's identity as a parent and her or his ability to maintain parental bonds. Toch (1975) did observe that incarceration and the consequent impairment of the incarcerated person's ability to contribute as a parent can result in feelings of guilt and shame.

Research, however, suggests that active engagement in parenting while in prison may provide stability for those who are incarcerated, which can reduce the psychological impact of imprisonment (Toch, 1975). Parenthood offers a useful way to engage people in prison on a number of issues such as substance abuse, steady employment, education, and even criminal behaviour in general because they do not want their children to engage in the same behaviours that resulted in their incarceration. People in prison begin to see themselves as behavioural models for their children and decide to change their lifestyle in order to set a positive example. By making the parental role the focus, the individual is seen as having an important role to play in the lives of others.

I've got the time, what can I do for you?

The concept of generativity encompasses many things. At some point, many adults recognize that they are what they leave behind. Therefore, they may be personally motivated to guide and teach the next generation. They may be motivated by social expectations of preparing younger generations for the future. Once an individual develops a concern for the next generation, she or he will also develop a belief in humankind. The individual will then be able to commit themselves to fulfil a generative role and engage in generative action. Finally, the individual will narrate their experiences promoting their generativity, thus providing coherence to their life story. This model of generativity outlines the ideal transformation to a generative adult. However, individuals of various circumstances arrive at Erikson's seventh stage of development. Arguably, ex-convicts and prison residents do not enjoy the freedom to naturally 'grow' across their lifespan. Indeed, incarceration offers barriers to the development of identity, intimacy, and generativity. Prisons encourage generative behaviours very little, which may lead people to experience feelings of stagnation rather than the positive feelings associated with 'giving back'. The research reviewed in this chapter refers almost exclusively to men. As seen in Chapter 2, the experiences and needs of women in prison are different to those of their male counterparts. Aspirations to generativity and generative actions may follow suit. I needed to gain a closer perspective. The research I embarked on is discussed next, including techniques of data collection and data analysis, and study limitations.

Research methods

Sample

I conducted interviews with 29 residents of the Kentucky Correctional Institution for Women (KCIW) in Pewee Valley, a unit of the Kentucky Department of Corrections (KDOC). I generated this sample using convenience sampling. Convenience sampling, which accesses research participants based on their availability, is widely used in qualitative research, especially when dealing with rare or hard-to-reach populations.

Given my geographic location in Knoxville, Tennessee, the Tennessee Department of Corrections (TDOC) was most convenient for me, and certainly more convenient than its Kentucky counterpart. However, TDOC was on a research freeze when I first embarked on data collection, in January 2008. The TDOC was not allowing any outside researcher to do research in any of their prison facilities and did not foresee an end to this ban soon. On learning of this obstacle, I approached the KDOC for research consideration. Upon contacting the KDOC, I felt encouraged by their gracious acceptance and assistance in seeking approval for the project. Pewee Valley was also close enough – four hours from my home – to allow for relative convenience in planning the interviews. Furthermore, Pewee Valley houses minimum to maximum security women, including one woman on death row at the time of this study. The diversity in criminal convictions, and thus the length of confinement could only be a boon to learning about the women's experiences and aspirations.

After KDOC emailed me with their approval for the research within the facility, I received an email from Shannon Butrum, Procedures Officer at the KCIW. She was assigned to recruit participants for me. Ms Butrum posted the research synopsis (see Appendix B) that I had provided, in the housing unit. When volunteers approached her concerning their interest, she scheduled interviews during the weeks that I would be visiting. The women were individually responsible for showing up to the appointment with me.

Interviews

My exploratory investigation extended to the question of whether the women would even express generative desires. Similarly, I wanted to know about what experiences in prison the women would mention as significant. As such, some sort of ethnography, which delves into experience and perspective, was indicated. Because my study mainly concerned individual experience and not social interaction, I did not opt to include a participant-observation component to the study. Hence, low-structure interviews were my method of choice.

After gaining KDOC's approval, I filed the necessary forms to receive human subjects, or Institutional Review Board (IRB), approval from the University of Tennessee. Having never been through this process before, I was struck by their concern for my safety in the interviewing process. I had to assure the IRB committee that I would not be endangered. Sight supervision by correctional officers provided the necessary assurance, and the project was approved.

I conducted one interview with each individual. Each interview lasted approximately two hours. Audio-recording devices were not allowed in the facility, so interviews were documented through careful note-taking – as much as possible. I wrote down direct quotes and especially particularly poignant statements. My interview notes averaged approximately 12 handwritten pages per participant. Following each interview I would expand on my notes, adding as much detail as I could recall.

The visitation room where I conducted all interviews was located in the administration building. This building was separate from the housing units and recreation building; thus it provided a private milieu away from the general population. While I never feared for my personal safety, the interview room was under video (not audio) – hence limited sight – surveillance. It was adequately secluded from staff interruptions and no guards were visible from where we were.

I initiated each interview with a greeting, whereby, I stood and shook the participant's hand, followed by a review of an informed consent form. Upon reading the highlights from the form, I allowed the participant time to read and sign the paper before proceeding with the interview. All of my participants readily signed the consent form with no concerns regarding the study and its procedures. I did have three participants specifically ask me the goal of the study, as they were interested in informing the public about women in prison.

Qualitative interviews are similar to conversations, if somewhat one-sided ones. I used several prompts and questions to generate dialogue with the participant. These are shown in no particular order in Table 4.1.

However, to a very large extent, I allowed my research participants to talk freely. I offered prompts when appropriate, but I did not redirect them to stay on point. As Seidman (1991) writes, 'The questions most used in an in-depth interview follow from what the participant has said' (p 69), and this was certainly true of my interviews. Even when the discussion reached far beyond my scope of research, I allowed the participant to continue talking – often discontinuing my note-taking to maintain more eye contact during especially intimate dialogue. For example, Katherine, a 50-year-old serving ten years for arson and insurance fraud, described the day her teenage

Table 4.1: Interview questions/prompts

Tell me about your life.

How is your relationship with other inmates?

Would you tell me about your children?

What is it like for you here?

How do you feel about ageing in prison?

What is your biggest regret?

What is your greatest contribution?

How do you see yourself when you get out?

What made you happy outside of prison?

Would you talk to me about older and younger inmates?

Do you consider yourself a victim, survivor, or offender?

Do you think about how you will be remembered?

Do you think about what, if any, legacy you will leave behind?

---

daughter died in a golf cart accident. She told me that she had never really talked about it before and later thanked me for listening. My reasoning for essentially relinquishing control of the interview was three-fold.

First, feminist scholars cite control over subjugated persons as problematic in research. The feminist ideal is to minimize power differentials, and I saw interrupting the women's talk as running counter to that goal. Second, due to the sensitive and personal nature of some of the stories my participants shared with me, I did not want to interrupt them and dismiss their stories as unimportant or bothersome. Third, because they were sharing intimate memories and emotions, I felt that allowing the women to take the discussion where they wished it to go, helped to establish rapport. I believed and believe that their willingness to share these stories with me indicated a certain amount of trust that I did not want to betray or belittle by discounting what they were telling me as straying from the focus of the interview.

Researchers acknowledge that even when both the interviewer and the respondent are women, differences persist that may affect the interviewing process. Power differentials between the interviewer and the participant affect the outcome of the interview (Giallombardo, 1966). I particularly enjoyed listening to several of the women. I found their strength, in the face of circumstances that I doubt I could overcome, to be remarkable. I also smiled and laughed with several jovial women who are clearly able to just take one day at a time. During the course of some of the interviews, my awareness of their incarceration faded until they adjusted their state-issued jacket or an announcement for cell count was made over the prison loudspeaker. I did not perceive any power differentials due in part, I believe, to the relatively unstructured format of the interview and my willingness to allow the women to discuss issues they felt were important.

Nonetheless, interviewing within a prison setting challenges the feminist vision of equality in research. Even before the interview, there is an inherent power differential as the interviewer is free and the interviewee is not. In one sense the researcher defines his or her own role in the field, but in another sense, it is defined for him or her by the situation and the perspective of the respondents (Giallombardo, 1966). I did not perceive any adverse effects on the interview data from my status as a free citizen and the women's status as incarcerated people. As mentioned before, I shook hands with each participant while introducing myself and then offered them a seat in a chair next to (and not opposite to) mine. As the majority of the participants were my seniors, I referred to them as 'ma'am' and showed them the same respect as I would for anyone else. I believe that my sincere show of respect helped to negate the power differential, even as my research cannot eliminate its structural basis.

Finally, interviewing older women *potentially* introduces a set of difficulties associated with the generation gap, such as a difference in familiarity with terminology. I was not aware of a generation gap during any of my interviews with older women and found them to be very easy to engage in conversation.

Methodological constraints

As a researcher, I encountered two major methodological constraints, both of which were institutionally imposed.

First, interviews were constrained by time, both in the sense that I had only two hours per interview and in the sense that I could only interview each woman once. While Pewee Valley was close enough to allow for easy access to the institution – 230 miles from my home – this distance, work, and family obligations at home required me to conduct multiple interviews in one day and to limit the interviewing period to two weeks. My two very young children, my very altruistic mother, and I 'holed up' in a motel near the facility for the duration – an arrangement that, given my mother's and my subsequent schedule, could not have easily been repeated. Therefore, within any one interview, I had to count on establishing rapport quickly in order to obtain the most information. I found that I did forge a connection with the majority of the participants. Several of the shorter interviews were with participants whom I observed to be sleepy and somewhat unresponsive to some of my prompts.

Second, by order of the KDOC, I was not permitted to use an audio recorder that would have allowed me to maintain more consistent eye contact with the participant and thus better facilitate the flow of conversation.

Although I encouraged participants to talk as they 'normally' would and assured them that I would be able to keep up with my notes, several of them felt the need to stop mid-story to allow my frantic note-taking a chance to catch up. An audio recorder would also have allowed me to get a word-for-word transcript of each interview. As it was, I was able to write down some direct quotes, but I was often forced to use short-hand and record more detailed notes following the end of the interview.

In general, people in prison are viewed as untrustworthy. In telling their stories, participants continually manage the impressions they make. In a sense, they perform by choosing to keep some secrets while disclosing others. Everyone, including prison residents, have some interest in 'saving face'. Therefore, participants are confronted with the dilemma of to tell or not to tell, to lie or not to lie during the interview (Goffman, 1963). For women in prison, their criminality is known to their families, other incarcerated people, guards, service providers, outside peers, and even strangers who have seen them on the news. While people in prison are viewed as being those with an unfavourable identity, it is important to note that all individuals use impression management. People in prison are not the only ones who tell narratives from their perspective (Girshick, 1999).

However, through this experience, I sensed that the women were honest with me. They were certainly forthcoming about their part in perpetrating harm, and as I explore in Chapter 7, they tended to take responsibility for their crimes. I felt gratified by the encounters, on both a personal level and from the perspective of the feminist goal of giving something back to our research participants. Some commented that the interview was therapeutic for them and that they came to some realizations about their past *through* the interview. Several participants cried during the interview while recounting particularly personal details, generally regarding their children. Stella, 52, referred to the interview as 'the closest thing we have to therapy'. A number of the participants expressed an interest in my research and requested a copy of the finished work. Informing the general public about the plight of incarceration for women, and in particular older women, was very important to them. Sue, who has served 21½ years of a life sentence, stated, "I hope this study helps somebody. This is the first one [study] I've ever signed up for in 21½ years. I thought it could help."

Analysis

Upon initially reviewing my data of analysis, I was at a loss. It seemed that everything my participants had said was fascinating and worthy of mention. I was not sure how to begin to organize the material into themes that would be informative or make sense. Thus began my complete immersion into the somewhat tedious task of data analysis. I gained a deep familiarity with the interview material through numerous readings and careful comparisons. After a time, I was able to identify multiple themes stemming from the narratives of my participants.

Namely, as somewhat expected, my participants talked about their children a good deal. Therefore, I began to look at patterns of mother/child relationships first. After focusing on the motherhood stories and struggles with their children, certain types of prison mothers became apparent. I then sought to name these patterns of experiencing older motherhood behind bars. I created as many pattern categories as ultimately described all of the mothers in the sample, or 27 of the 29.

Next, I was interested in how age, which by now I knew to be an important factor in the experience of motherhood behind bars, would affect the other aspects of prison life. This search through the data brought me to the notion of acceptance – of incarceration, of responsibility, and themselves.

Finally, I studied evidence of generativity, my initial interest and focus. While I had expected to hear some interest in giving back to society, such as plans to lecture youth on the dangers of drugs, I had not expected the zealousness with which my participants discussed their plans for future acts of generativity. I also did not expect the number of generative opportunities within the prison institution.

I now turn to these research findings. In the three chapters that follow, I report on the realities, emotions, hardships, and joys shared by the women of Pewee Valley.

5

Parenting Behind Bars

About two thirds of women in prison are mothers of children under the age of 18, and most of those mothers were living with their children prior to their incarceration (Bureau of Justice and Statistics, 2000). Therefore, any researcher who seeks to understand the 'typical' woman in prison must consider that she is a mother and, more specifically, a mother to young children. In one respect, my study accords with such an assumption; that is, 27 of the 29 women in my sample, including 25 of the older women, were mothers. However, given the older mean age of my sample, it creates a unique picture of parenting from prison, as 25 of the 27 were mothers of adult children living on their own.

It was very common for the women I interviewed to speak about their children. While several of my prompts directly pertained to issues of motherhood and one's children (for example, Would you tell me about your children?), 26 of the women initiated discussions about their children voluntarily or in response to the generativity-related prompts (for example, Do you think about how you will be remembered?). The frequency with which the women in my sample talked about their children is not surprising given that incarcerated mothers have, in earlier studies, stressed the importance of their children (Owen, 1998) and the pain caused by separation (Morash and Schram, 2002). Advocates for the incarcerated population and, more recently, researchers in academia have become concerned about the challenges posed for people in prison, children, and families by parental incarceration (for example, Fox, 1984; Fletcher and Moon, 1993; Owen, 1998; Enos, 2001; Easterling, Feldmeyer, and Presser 2021). Much of the research on incarcerated parents, primarily mothers, focuses on their children (Baunach, 1985; Bloom and Steinhart, 1993; Siegal, 2011) – generally either their placement during their mother's incarceration or their ability to cope with it. Extensive research has linked maternal incarceration with depression in both mothers and children under the age of 18 (Koban, 1983; Henriques, 1996; Sharp and Marcus-Mendoza, 2001; Siegal, 2011). Family systems are stressed by even short periods of separation. Research primarily illuminates the emotional and behavioural problems of younger children as a result of their mother's incarceration, but it rarely addresses such things as pertain to having *adult* children on the outside.

While all of the 27 research participants who were mothers reported that separation from their children was difficult, the nature and severity of the difficulty they described varied. To better understand this diversity, I considered the nuances of the mother/child bond as reported by my research participants. I took into account not only their responses to the question concerning what it is like to be a mother in prison but also the *manner* in which the women discussed their relationships with their children. Over the course of each interview, the women tended to recount the evolution of their relationship with their children over time. They generally followed a narrative pattern of discussing how things were, how things are, and how they want things to be where their children are concerned.

I identified four types of older mothers in prison. The *remorseful mother* regrets her past mistakes as a young mother and hopes now to reconcile with her children. The *contented mother* enjoys a strong relationship with her children and reports being relatively content with her incarceration. The *uneasy mother* worries about the well-being of her children during the separation. Finally, the *abandoned mother* is surprised and saddened by her children's thoughtlessness during her incarceration. Clearly, the experience of parenting older children from behind bars is variable. The nature of the relationship with their children prior to incarceration has a significant influence on the nature of their relationship during incarceration.

In this chapter, I examine the women's perspectives on mothering from behind bars. In so doing, I attempt to piece together their accounts of their parenting and their plans for the same. Most of my participants voiced concern over the impact of their incarceration on family members, particularly their children. The women discussed their appreciation for family and described the nature of and hope for their relationships with their grandchildren.

The remorseful mother

For my older research participants – those 40 years of age and older – raising children was an activity described in the past tense. That is, their children had already been raised: either they or others had done so. As they spoke to me, they were likely to recall not only their past behaviours, such as drug use or solicitation, but also to comment on the effects that such habits had clearly had on their children. The ability to identify instances of long-term effects of their behaviour on their children is not an ability afforded to younger people with younger children. So while younger people in prison may indeed recognize 'how bad' incarceration and separation are for their young children, their perspective is largely limited to the present. Yet, many of my older participants recalled their reported deficiencies as younger mothers without prompting.

Ten of the older women said that their biggest regret was not having been able or willing to raise their children in the past. While their incarceration provoked remorse and regret in specific regard to their children, for many, the damage had been done. Seventeen of the older women I interviewed related their past behaviours to the struggles and emotional distress *currently* experienced by their adult children. Eight out of the 17 reported strained or estranged relationships with their adult children and desired to reconcile with them. They criticized their shortcomings and attributed their currently 'objective' insight to time, which is abundantly afforded in prison, and to simply getting older. Because recollections of the past were laden with regret, I refer to this category as the *remorseful mother*. As a mother of adult children, the remorseful mother is able to witness the consequences of her behaviours on her children and typically desires to re-establish the relationships with them that were either damaged or lost.

Frances, a 53-year-old White woman, for example, considered her children's struggles in adulthood and her strained relationships with them to be a reflection of her failure to guide and nurture them as children. Frances initiated a discussion about her sons five times during the interview. Each time, she either lamented not providing enough love and care for them as children or voiced concern about not being with them at present.

Gina:	What is your biggest regret?
Frances:	Not being a better mother to my boys. Not showing enough love. My youngest son said, 'The TV became my mommy.' I didn't see that. I was getting high. I was selfish. I blame myself. That's why they [my children] are struggling like they are.
Gina:	Struggling how?
Frances:	My oldest is getting a divorce and my youngest is in jail.

Frances mentioned her oldest son and his perception of her not showing him enough love three separate times. She considered her mistakes as a mother as contributing to his divorce. Although Frances was incarcerated after her children were grown, she said that she spent most of their childhood addicted to drugs and associating with the 'wrong crowd' – that is, other people who used drugs. Her children were not her priority then, but she stated that they are her priority now.

Gina:	How do you see yourself when you get out?
Frances:	Scared, but excited. I want to enjoy the rest of my life. I want to be with my husband (she married while incarcerated).

> I want to spend time with my boys. I want to sit down with the oldest and let him know how much he is loved. I didn't realize how much I hurt him. I want a big family – to be surrounded by family. That comes with ageing for me.

Frances, like 16 other older women I spoke with, was no longer the mother of young children. Frances believed she was witnessing the consequences of her poor parenting in the past. Therefore, Frances exemplifies two evidently common tendencies among the older participants in my sample – that of being cognizant of the effect one's lifestyle had on one's children and desiring to make amends for one's past mistakes.

Sue, a 54-year-old White woman, provided a similar account of recognition and remorse. Sue has served 21½ years of a life sentence, so her children were young when she first entered prison. She talked about her children multiple times during the interview, but she depicted her relationships with them as strained.

Gina:	Would you tell me about your children?
Sue:	My middle child, my son, is in prison for ten years. We are in touch. He was young when I was arrested. So getting someone to bring them here was hard. I developed some emotional detachment to avoid the pain. My daughter visited three years ago. I don't know where she is now. I think she's had a nervous breakdown. Her husband left her. I think she doesn't want to deal with me. I know my children love me. I've hurt them. I was very self-centered at one time.
Gina:	Do you want things to change?
Sue:	Of course. My children are very important to me. I hope to re-establish bonds.

At the time of the interview, Sue described herself as personable, caring, compassionate, and goal-oriented. Recalling the time of her arrest, Sue said, "I was beaten down – all the domestic violence and now a human being was dead." Sue's abusive partner kidnapped, raped, and murdered a woman he 'picked up' off the street. Sue was in the car at the time and did not try to stop it. She said she feared her partner would have killed her too. For Sue, her experience with domestic violence and drug addiction affected the way she treated her children, but she claimed responsibility for her parenting as in the following exchanges:

Gina:	What is your biggest regret?
Sue:	The way I raised my kids – not setting a better example for them by raising them right.

Later in the interview, Sue acknowledged her pride in her children.

Gina: What is your greatest contribution?
Sue: Nothing ... no wait... having my kids.

Sue discussed her children, unprompted, two more times during the interview. She stated that her family was the biggest victim of her incarceration and shared, "I can't do anything about that, but we can move forward." Sue did indeed look forward. When I asked her what she thinks about, she reported most often thinking about her grandchildren, children, and freedom.

Sue's personality and demeanour struck me as consistent with how movies portray prison 'old-timers'. That is, she seemed laid back, but she also conveyed a wisdom that seemed to come from years of self-evaluation and contemplation, perhaps nurtured by seven years of counselling with the prison chaplain – someone she described as instrumental in helping her 'turn her life around'. Sue demonstrates a dichotomy shared with seven of the women I interviewed. That is, her greatest contribution and her biggest regret both pertained to her children.

Guilt was a recurring theme for Clara, a 65-year-old White woman serving 530 years for sodomy, first-degree incest and other related charges. To better understand Clara's relationships with her children, it is important to grasp her complex story of false accusations and family disruption. According to Clara, after her mother died she became deeply depressed. Her house was dirty and her sons were placed in foster care. At the time, the foster parents wanted to adopt both of her sons, and she believed the foster parents manipulated the situation by telling her oldest son what to say. Her son's accusations of sodomy and incest resulted in more than 79 charges against her and her husband. Clara claimed there was no physical evidence, but that she and her husband were convicted based on the word of her son, not facts. The oldest son now feels guilty and wants to 'make things right'. Clara is currently jointly appealing her conviction along with her husband, who is serving the same sentence. Clara said she never blamed her son and stated that part of her determination to 'fix things' was that she was getting older and she did not want her son to carry the guilt of making false allegations for the rest of his life.

Clara further reported that her daughter harboured some resentment towards her for the dissolution of the family and, consequently, has not contacted her in 18 years (since Clara first entered prison). She lamented, "I wish I had told my oldest daughter I loved her more. ... I would be kinder, if I could do it over, again. You don't realize you're hurting anything."

Clara recognized her shortcomings as a mother when her children were younger and hoped that by overturning her and her husband's convictions, they would be able to forge new relationships with their children. Likewise,

Frances lamented her mistakes when she was a young mother, but she was also particularly aware of the effect her mistakes had on her children as adults. Thus, she felt most guilty about not being with them now. "I should be out there with my boys. They both need me now." Sue's children were young when she was first incarcerated. By her admission, her renewed appreciation for family and desire for forgiveness took time. She said she now wanted to tell her children, "Please let me back in your life, even though I don't deserve it." The regret, the guilt, and the desire to repair the damage caused by their deficiencies as young mothers epitomize the remorseful mother.

The contented mother

The positive appraisals of one's ongoing relationship with grown children were mainly voiced by women who were not incarcerated until later in life or by women who were able to maintain consistent contact with their children over the years. Approximately 16 of the 27 women with children were incarcerated for the first time after the age of 40 and after their children were grown. All 16 reported close relationships with their adult children. An additional four women were incarcerated when their children were still young but were able to maintain contact and establish close relationships with their now-adult children.

Overall, 17 of the 27 women who had children reported having good relationships with them. Therefore, maintaining adequate, while perhaps not ideal, contact with one's adult children was not unusual for the women in this study. Few of the women I interviewed complained about the (low) frequency of contact with their children. I speculate that since adult children are able to take care of themselves, the women would, arguably, not enjoy daily or perhaps even monthly contact with their children if they were in free society so that incarceration was less an obstruction to maintaining close bonds with their children than it was for younger mothers. Good relationships between adult children and parents do not require frequent face-to-face contact – something that research regarding incarcerated mothers with young children considers vital to maintaining a strong relationship.

Continuing contact with their children may be the most significant predictor of an individual in prison's' chances of reuniting their families upon release (Girshick, 1999). Of course, this presumption stands to reason because mothers of younger children are often the sole caregiver to their children prior to incarceration. Therefore, the abrupt termination of family routine can be most devastating to both parties. Mothers generally worry about losing their children's love (Baunach, 1985). Concerning the plight of the younger mother I can only offer two examples from my sample: from the three younger women I interviewed, only two had children under the age of 18. Both of my participants with younger children reported fairly frequent visits. Sarah, a 27-year-old Black woman, had two children currently living with her parents who she reported seeing every week. Christy, a 34-year-old White woman, also said she receives regular visits from her two children. While both Sarah and Christy described close relationships with their children, they also mentioned uneasiness in having to relinquish parental control to those who were currently caring for their children. Frequent visits were an important way for them to remain in their children's lives, but such was not the case for women with adult children.

Five of the older women in my sample reported that while they continued to miss being with their families and looked forward to reuniting with them upon their release, they were *content* with their current situation. For me, these women typified what I call the *contented mother*. The contented mother is able to maintain contact with her children throughout their childhood and to continue positive relations with their children as adults. Women in this category were generally either serving long sentences or getting ready to be released; thus, the contented mother either reconciles herself to the reality of a long separation or takes comfort in an upcoming release date. Either way, the existence of a supportive family unit gives the woman a sense of security and allows her to better deal with her incarceration.

Rose, a 60-year-old Black woman, affectionately called 'Granny' by the other residents, offers a good example of positive family relations. I encountered Rose's charming nature as she smiled, laughed, and called me 'baby girl'. Rose was serving a 13-year sentence for manslaughter. She told me that her abusive husband was accidentally shot in the head while they were wrestling over a gun. She had served a year and a half of her sentence and claimed, "now that I know God is with me, I'm doing fine."

Gina:	What made you happy outside of prison?
Rose:	Being with my daughter, son, and family – my two kids and four grandsons, my little family – I enjoyed going shopping for them and going to ballgames. I did all that with them, played video games with them.
[Pause]	
Rose:	I appreciate being with family more now than when I was younger. When I was younger, I was doing other things. I'm more happy now with family – since I'm older. Now I just want to sew and crochet and play with grandsons. My daughter wants me to live with her. I think she doesn't want me to live by myself. My grandsons will want me to go go go. I probably will live with her.

Rose reported that she was close to her two children and four grandsons, and that "it has killed them since I've been here, but I tell them that I will be home again." Rose said she raised her children "old-timey", which I interpreted to mean family-oriented. Rose reported she was content because prison forced her to examine herself and her path of self-destruction. She declared, "I would have gotten AIDS if this hadn't happened. God knew what He was doing. I wanted to kill myself – now I've got peace of mind." She credited prison with her 'recovery' by helping her to recognize her abuse and to overcome her sadness. According to Rose, "When you have peace of mind, it's as sweet as blackberry juice." Women, like Rose, who were assured of their children's well-being seemed to be the most tolerant of their own incarceration. Rose exemplified something that younger women in prison often do not understand but admire; that is, the ability to do 'easy time' – defined by my participants as not stressing about the outside world while in prison.

Rose's easy time seemed to follow from the comfort she took in knowing she had a place to live with her daughter upon release. Several of the women I spoke with talked about where they would live after they were released. The women who were incarcerated for the first time after their children were grown and were assured of their children's well-being took some comfort in knowing they had someone to take care of them upon their release. Like Rose, a few reported that their children wanted them to live with them. Mable, a prison first-timer stated:

Mable: My sons are arguing over me to stay with them, but I told them that they have families of their own.
Gina: So where will you go when you get out?
Mable: I'll probably go back to Indiana to be closer to my sons and grandson, but I want to get back on my own feet.

Very different was May, a 50-year-old Black woman serving 12 years for trafficking cocaine. She expressed anger with her children for 'leaving her for dead' during her incarceration. She seemed to feel particularly betrayed by one daughter with whom she had lived before. She stated, "I'll need a place to stay when I get out. My daughter's boyfriend is staying with her. What about me? I have no place to go. There's nobody else in my family. That's bad. I have no place to go."

With the time of raising their children behind them, many of the older participants I interviewed now anticipated that their children would care for them. Thus, the age-graded reversal of caregiver and receiver roles – from parent to child, then child to parent – common in free society is not negated but is perhaps amplified through incarceration and the mother's difficulties in starting over. Three of the women I interviewed specifically stated that starting over scared them. For example, I asked Eve, a long-termer, what she will do when she gets out. She replied, "The world will be so changed.

I do not know my children (whom she gave up for adoption). My family will be dead – nobody left. That scares me. This is my home. I don't want it to be, but it is." Dependable relationships with their children gave the women I spoke with a sense of security and eased some fears of starting over upon their release, a luxury that is not afforded to incarcerated women who have no children.

Family was a major theme for Sally, a 46-year-old White woman, who shared that she was very dependent on her family for support. Whereas boredom with her life after her children were grown, led her to 'partying' with 'the wrong crowd' and using drugs, she longed to return to the comforts of being a housewife – the lifestyle she had known prior to using drugs. Saying, "my kids are my life," Sally took great comfort in her family's support. "My husband takes care of me. My son bought me a TV and my daughter writes to me."

Gina: How do you see yourself when you get out?
Sally: I have a new grandbaby. I'll spend time with her and my family. I want to help my daughter – set up a business with her. I don't want to do drugs anymore. My husband lined up aftercare [drug counseling]. He has moved out of the old area now.
Gina: How do you feel?
Sally: I feel older now, stronger-minded now. But I feel like a grandmother. I feel content. I don't want to hurt [emotionally] my husband anymore.

Sally admitted to counting the days until her parole hearing, which was scheduled later in the month of the interview. She said prison made her stop and realize what she was doing to herself and her family. She learned to focus on positives instead of negatives. For Sally, her family was a positive source for her. Sally was content because she was a mother and a grandmother who anticipated a happy future of family love and support.

Misty, a 50-year-old White woman serving a life sentence for first-degree murder, also enjoyed strong family support and provided a good example of maintaining family contact during lengthy incarceration. She reported that she receives weekly visits from and makes daily phone calls to family members because they live close to the prison. She described herself as having a "charming personality" and being spiritual and very family-oriented.

Gina: What is the most difficult thing about being in prison?
Misty: Still being away from family after 23 years.
Gina: How do you see yourself when you get out?
Misty: I want to be with family, just be with my family.

Misty admitted that what she referred to as her 'spiritual' transition took time. She stated, "A lot goes on in prison. I've changed, gotten older, and gotten more spiritual. I wanted to change. I wanted something different for my family." Misty initiated discussions about her family seven times during the interview. She reported her biggest regret was "not being woman enough" to raise her children, recalling that during many years of drug addiction, her mother raised them. While she stated that she was not happy being in prison, she reported that she was "content."

Gina: What is prison like for you?
Misty: Coming here has made me the individual I am today. If I was still out there, I would have been dead. I like who I am today. I told my mom this the other day.

Misty used the term 'content' several times. She stated, "God brought me peace to deal with what was going on." Misty may never be released from prison, but she is content because as she stated, "my family believes in me." Misty is one of five women I interviewed who were serving life sentences. Of these women, she had served the most years and reported the most frequent contact with her family. Misty was not typical in her circumstances, but she demonstrated patience, endurance, and determination – which were common characteristics of the women in my sample. Similarly, Rose and Sally gained strength from the support they received from their families; thus, they seemed better able to contend with their current incarceration.

The uneasy mother

Some of the research participants who reported having close relationships with their children also regarded incarceration as an obstacle which both mother and child must endure. Many of the women I interviewed mentioned particular hardships suffered by, or complaints, in excess of simply missing them, made by their children due to separation. Twelve of the women I spoke with reported close relationships with their children and shared that their children were having a particularly difficult time with their absence. Generally, these women had more or less accepted their incarceration, but their children had not.

For many of the women, their children's inability to cope with the separation was a main concern and source of worry during their incarceration, inhibiting a sense of contentment. In general, these women had had frequent interaction with their children before their incarceration. Their routine was rudely interrupted. I refer to the women in this category as the *uneasy mother*. The uneasy mother is able to maintain contact with her children throughout their childhood and to continue positive relations with their children as adults. However, while the mothers may have adjusted to their incarceration, their children seemingly had not; thus, the uneasy mother is anxious to resume her role in free society – generally as caregiver either to adult children who have remained emotionally or financially dependent and/or to elderly parents who require assistance. Thus, women who were charged with caring for older parents prior to their incarceration are also included in this category. It is also in this category that I classify my three younger participants.

Two of the younger women had minor children who were being raised by close family members. Their adjustment and the adjustment of their children supported previous research in that they were anxious to return to their children and resume parental responsibility. Christy, 34, reported that her teenage daughter now seeks advice and guidance from her (Christy's) sister. While Christy said she was close to her sister, she lamented not being readily available to her daughter. Thus, like several of the older women, my younger participants were worried and concerned about their children, which prevented them from feeling contentment during their incarceration.

Separation from her daughter, whom she refers to as her 'best friend', was a prominent theme for Polly, 44; so too were the pains of being a mother from behind bars.

Gina: What is it like being a mother in prison?
Polly: Pure plain and simple: it is horrible. Can you imagine losing contact with your mother?

Polly is serving a 15-year sentence for assault. She had been drinking when she fell with her infant step-grandchild getting him out of the crib. She told me she already had back problems and nerve damage at the time of the incident. The baby stopped breathing and she shook him to revive him. According to Polly, the baby suffered no permanent damage.

Gina: Have you forgiven yourself?
Polly: That's a hard one. I'm struggling with it. I'm trying to forgive myself. I loved that child like he was my own. I'll never drink, again. I know that.

For Polly, prison "stopped her from making excuses." She stated "I wouldn't accept I was an alcoholic. Now, I can." Polly was most concerned about the well-being of her daughter. She reported that her daughter visits with her two grandchildren, but she knows her daughter is suffering with her incarceration. "My daughter is my best friend – always has been. It may be worse for her, that's the worst part. I almost wish they [my family] could forget me until I get out. My daughter is having a rough time right now. We would always shop and bake together."

Polly and the 11 other women I spoke with expressed great concern for their children's ability to cope with their absence. In Polly's case, her normal routine of frequently being with her daughter and sharing daily experiences was interrupted; thus, Polly reported being more concerned for her daughter than herself.

Similarly, Evelyn lamented not being able to physically be there to help her children, of whom she was quite proud, during hard times. One day her daughter told her, "Mom, you just don't understand. You're not here anymore." Evelyn is 44 years old and has currently served 12 years of a 70-year sentence for murder and attempted murder. Evelyn said, "My first alcohol blackout was at seven – my mother hit me and I couldn't feel it. I knew I would be an alcoholic before I knew what it was."

Gina: Do you have any contact with your mother now?
Evelyn: My mother quit drinking. We have the best relationship ever now. We've worked on a lot of stuff.

While under the influence of alcohol, Evelyn killed one person and attempted to kill another person who had recently beaten her mother. She said she remembered coming out of a bar and then waking up in jail.

Evelyn was sexually abused multiple times as a child and physically abused by boyfriends, one of whom broke several bones in her face. Yet, Evelyn declared, "I've survived everything. I have scars all over from abuse and now I'm a recovering alcoholic and drug addict." Evelyn struck me as strong-willed – a survivor. She, however, praised her children for their own determination and successes. Her son is an engineer and her daughter is a nurse. I asked her how she feels about being a mother in prison:

Evelyn: I'm not out there so how can I tell them what they can or can't do. So, I'm more like sharing what I feel. You lose your authority as a mother – makes it hard to swallow. [Prison] strips you of all your power when you come here. ... You're limited, but can still keep some power with little children. ... Not when they are older. My daughter had an abortion, when she came here I couldn't hold her. My daughter said if you don't make parole, I'll stop believing in God. I said God has a bigger plan. Maybe I need to be here for somebody in here. I try to make things positive not negative.

Evelyn reported that she was recently given a 20-year deferment by the parole board. She was not as concerned with how she would handle 20 more years as she was worried about her children. Evelyn's experience spoke of the struggles of motherhood behind bars. Whereas she had accepted the terms of her incarceration, her children continued to suffer; thus, she did as well.

For Jane, family well-being was a daily source of stress and worry. Jane was serving 15 years in prison for second-degree manslaughter. Jane recounted her abusive husband, in a drunken state, saying he was going to shoot somebody and threatened Jane's family. The two fought over his gun and Jane's husband was shot in the shoulder. He did not want to press charges, but he later died due to complications from the injury. His sister pressed charges and Jane was arrested. Jane said, "My kids and mother were furious. I had taken a plea. Mom said I should have gone to trial and told them about my husband's abuse, but I didn't want to do that to my kids." Jane had served almost two years of her sentence at the time of the interview.

Gina: What do you think about the most?
Jane: I try to look toward the future. Getting out. I'm not sure my mom will be there or my handicapped daughter. My daughter has grand mal seizures. She is on baby food now. I think about not being there. When I call and get no answer, it scares me. If something happens to my mom, my daughter will die too. She has only ever been with my mom since my incarceration.

While 25 of the 29 women in my sample were mothers of adult children, Jane's situation was unique. Prior to her incarceration, she was the caregiver to her disabled adult daughter. Currently, her daughter is living with Jane's 84-year-old mother.

Gina: How do you see your life when you get out?
Jane: I hope Mom and my daughter are still here. I'll take care of them. I want to let Mom have some rest. My grandson was ten years old when I was locked up. He'll be 19 when I get out. I miss them, but I hate seeing them. When they leave, it's more depressing. I'm not there to be involved in everything. I miss that. Whether good or bad, I want to be with them. I've always had a close-knit family. I pray God keeps them all healthy. Mom still cares for my handicapped daughter. People from church come and help her. She has support, and Mom is a strong woman.

Jane mentioned her concern for the well-being of her daughter and her mother three times during the interview. She told me that she was recently denied parole.

Gina: How do you feel about the denial?
Jane: I thought I was going to get out. I didn't want to call my family. They are the ones being punished. I wanted to get out and give my mom some golden years.

Jane's family lives in Texas, which makes visitation virtually impossible for her disabled daughter and elderly mother. Instead, she calls, writes, and hopes they will both be there upon her release.

A 2020 American Association of Retired Persons (AARP) survey revealed that more than one fifth (21 per cent) of Americans are unpaid caregivers, with 17 per cent of them providing supportive services to their parents or other older relatives (Schoch, 2020). Primary caregivers to elders are most commonly middle-aged women who provide hands-on care and emotional support, and share their homes with their older parents (Dellmann-Jenkins, Blankemeyer, and Pinkard, 2000). As the number of adults over age 65 is expected to double in the next 40 years, with the most rapidly growing segment being those aged 85 and older (Bronfenbrenner et al, 1996), the importance of the care that family caregivers provide for an increasing portion of the population becomes clear. Eleven of the women I interviewed mentioned their parents. Eve, a long-termer, did not anticipate leaving prison while her father was still alive. She reported, "I do everything to say life is great in here. I don't want him to worry." Sue was concerned about her mother's health. She said, "My mom had a heart attack. She is in a nursing home. I hope she lives until I get out." In general, the women reported close relationships with their parents and were generally interested in 'giving them a break' from having to care for them or their children during their incarceration.

The abandoned mother

By its very nature, incarceration challenges the parental role and threatens the mother-child bond. Six of the women I interviewed were preoccupied with strained relationships or worrying about the whereabouts and well-being of their grown children. These women appeared most troubled and ill at ease about being incarcerated and unable to be with their children. I also spoke with women who may have been incarcerated when their children were still young or for various other reasons were not able to effectively raise their children. Two of these women had never had close relationships with their children so contact was non-existent or very sporadic. Two of the women I spoke with said they were close with their children but felt betrayed or alarmed by the lack of contact during incarceration. I call the women in this group the *abandoned mother*. The abandoned mother is often overtly worried about the well-being of her children or harbours some resentment for the lack of support. While the mothers may have adjusted to incarceration, they reported some concern and anxiety about their children.

Doris has served two months of a one-year sentence for prescription forgery and her worry and concern for her daughter was a major theme during her interview. She talked frequently about her daughter who she had not seen since her incarceration. This was her first time in prison and her first time in any kind of trouble with the law. Doris was in a wheelchair and dependent on other people to move her around on campus. Her daughter and grandchildren were living in her house, but she was not able to call (due to a block on her daughter's phone) to reassure herself of their well-being.

Gina: Do you have any contact with your daughter?
Doris: No, I don't know why she doesn't even write.
Gina: Were you close before you came here?
Doris: I thought so. I haven't seen her since my arrest. I know she loved me. It is just not like her to let me come in somewhere and not even write.

Doris described herself as friendly and helpful. While Doris said she had always had a lot of friends, she stated, "I won't have that many when I go home. All of them are very righteous and judgemental. I didn't think about that until I came here." Doris related that her friends do not understand why she committed her crime, nor can they understand her addiction to prescription drugs. For Doris, prison life was "pretty much okay", but she was concerned with her daughter's behaviour and anxious to be released for that reason.

Doris expected to be paroled a month after the interview. She was quite concerned about her daughter but also seemed sad for herself. Doris was unique in that she assumed she and her daughter were close and expected support but was surprised to receive none. Her situation exemplifies the isolation experienced by some women during their incarceration.

Likewise, May, a 50-year-old Black woman, anticipated financial and emotional support from her three daughters. Yet, she said that her children had not contacted her or supported her in any way during her incarceration. She felt hurt and betrayed by her loved ones on the outside.

Gina: Would you tell me about your children?
May: My oldest wrote me one time. My baby girl didn't write at all. My middle child (with whom Mary lived with during last parole leave) sent me my Social Security checks. As far as I'm concerned, they sent me nothing. They don't write me. I cried about that. I always provided for them. I'm not writing them no more. They never write me back. I'm leaving them. They

	won't have to worry about me. They'll miss me. I babysat, cleaned house, but they left me for dead. I still bought them a lot.
Gina:	Will you call them?
May:	I shouldn't have to. I'm their mother. I still love them but won't buy them nothing. I mean it. I'm saying it from my heart. I've prayed about it. I won't give them nothing. I can make it another year in here.

May was angry at her daughters, but she was anxious to reunite with her grandchildren. It was not uncommon for the women I spoke with to desire to return to the way things were prior to their incarceration but to want to be even more involved than before. May stated, "I'm learning in here. I can help my grandkids with homework. That makes me proud. I couldn't do that before."

Gina:	How do you see yourself when you get out?
May:	My priority will be my grandkids. ... I'm changing. I'm a better person than I was. I'm learning with my schooling to help them. I was a good grandmother then and am now. They knew I was selling drugs. ... They knew I lied about not being able to play with them. I feel bad about lying to this day. No more drugs for me. I will take them on vacations that I've never been. I want to take them myself.

In general, all the older research participants shared that it was difficult not to be able to spend more time with their grandchildren. For all of them, talking about being a grandmother and being with them upon release seemed to bring joy.

Gina:	What made you feel good before incarceration?
May:	Drugs. No pain. I just wanted fast money. I dealt Monday through Friday and on weekends, I used.
Gina:	What will replace that feeling for you when you get out?
May:	My grandkids. I will be there and more. Bring on the fun. When before I told them to wait. I won't do that anymore. I will take them places and be there for them. But I won't give my daughters nothing.

May looked forward to her future despite epitomizing the abandoned mother because of the joy and optimism associated with being a grandmother.

For Mary, suspicion and uncertainty were recurring themes. She was serving five years for possession of a controlled substance and lived in the mental health support living unit. She seemed very excited and was quite talkative throughout the interview. It appeared to me that Mary had yet to face her demons. I asked her if she thought she might use drugs again upon her release. The following was her reply:

> 'I can't do drugs – something tragic would have to happen. I'll be in the same environment, but can't go back to [the] same people. All of the town knows me. All of the drug dealers know me. They'll follow me. You get to thinking about it. If you think about doing wrong, you might as well do it.'

Mary was very worried about her daughter and she repeatedly discussed her fears and concerns about her. Mary discussed being a mother from prison.

> 'I think she [my daughter] might be into something. She's smart but dating a no-good guy. I wrote her a three-page letter. I don't want her to move too fast. I told her, "He'll use you." My daughter is not looking right. I'm worried. I'm being a mom from here as best I can. My daughter has Power of Attorney. She spent my money. I don't know where it went. I'm scared. She's never been away from me. We've always been together. I don't want her to suffer. I'll tell her not to go wrong, but I'm not there to see her.'

Mary could also be critical of her daughter:

> 'I want her to do something – get a good job. I need to take care of myself. I'm tired of supporting her. My daughter is old enough to take care of herself, but I am concerned about my grandkids. I don't want her to do to them what I did to her. I feel like my daughter has been taking advantage of me.'

Mary said she planned to spend more time with her family. "Go places with them. Before, I was just getting high." I grouped Mary in the category of abandoned mother because of her suspicions about her daughter. While they have a reasonably close relationship, the nature of that relationship changed with Mary's incarceration and she no longer seemed to trust her daughter. Mary demonstrates a level of vulnerability; that is, financial dependence, that comes with incarceration, but one which is only problematic if exploited by someone on the outside.

Then there was Stella, a 52-year-old White woman serving three years for robbery, who appeared very sad and visibly depressed. Stella reported that she had been in and out of mental hospitals many times. She was diagnosed as bipolar schizophrenic and has always been on multiple medications. She was emotionally unable to raise her children and gave them up for adoption long before her incarceration. She remarked that she has always, "pushed people who loved me away. I've never been married. I gave kids up to other people because I wanted them to have a good home – I never had one." Stella has attempted suicide multiple times outside of prison. She has recently been in touch with her two oldest children, but the relationship is strained at best. She stated:

> 'I'm hoping, during clean times, my kids will come around. It won't be strong relationship, but it will be a start. I am older now and so are they – they should be able to understand it better. They are in their 30s now and know more about life than they did in their 20s.'

She continued, "The closest I'll be to them is an associate, not even a close friend." Stella believed that her troubles, such as drugs and depression, came with giving up her children. Thus, Stella may be seen as a self-inflicted abandoned mother as she admitted to always alienating people. Stella declared that she is now tired of being alone.

For Stella, life was lonely, prison life was lonely, but she hoped that somehow she would not experience such loneliness after release. While abandoned, Stella had not anticipated that her children would visit or support her during her incarceration as she reported to only recently have begun to initiate contact. On the other hand, Doris, May, and Mary expected their children to care about them and show some financial and emotional support during their incarceration, but were saddened and, for some, angry when their children disregarded them.

Mothering and grandmothering from state prison

Previous research has established the strain on young motherhood caused by incarceration, but the experiences of incarcerated mothers of *adult* children and the effects of incarceration on grandparenting have received little attention. While most of my participants lamented the impacts of their earlier criminal behaviours on their children, their experience of incarceration varied depending on the nature of their *current* mother/child relationship. The nature of the relationship with their children prior to incarceration had a significant influence on the nature of their relationship during incarceration.

I classified my participants into four categories of older mothers in prison. The *remorseful mother* was either incarcerated while her children were young or in some other way engaged in deviant behaviour while they were growing up. In either case, the remorseful mother felt that she had failed to effectively raise her children. Therefore, she now seeks to reconcile with her children as adults. The *contented mother* was generally incarcerated for the first time after her children were grown and had forged a close relationship with them when they were younger. As such, their relationship had endured and the contented mother now enjoys financial and/or emotional support from her children during her incarceration. Overall, the contented mother reported being content with her current circumstances because she was assured that her family would be there for her upon her release. The *uneasy* mother worries about the well-being of her children during her incarceration. The mother had typically adjusted to the separation, but her adult children, often still relatively dependent on her, had not. Thus, the uneasy mother became distracted and concerned about her children's well-being during her incarceration. Finally, the *abandoned mother* is surprised and saddened by her children's disregard during her incarceration. The abandoned mother does not have the comfort of knowing her children are waiting for her when she is released, so incarceration generally becomes a lonely and, perhaps scary, experience. Clearly, the experience of parenting older children from behind bars is variable. Incarcerated mothers of adult children do not 'do their time' in the same manner as mothers of young children, nor is there a universal experience among older mothers.

The grandmothers, while sad about not being with their grandchildren, typically discussed grandparenting as something to look forward to upon their release. May, one of the abandoned mothers, had turned her attention to her grandchildren rather than her children: the role of grandmother still held excitement for her. Research has found that women are more invested in their roles as grandparents than men (Troll, 1983; Aldous, 1995). Family appears to gain heightened importance for adults starting at middle age, so grandparents might derive a sense of their life's accomplishment for the first time through their grandchildren (Erikson, Erikson, and Kivnick, 1986).

A word is also in order about the two childless women in my sample. Peggy, a 58-year-old White woman, said she felt alone. "I don't have anybody. I have no children. No one takes care of me." She despaired of starting over at her age. "I feel like my life is over. I feel so old. I don't want to get old by myself." Very different from Peggy was Elle, a 51-year-old Black woman. Elle told me that she receives financial support from her boyfriend and has an abundance of emotional support from her friends from church. Not having children caused her no suffering. In their uniqueness and the obvious need for human connection, the experiences of incarceration for women without children are not unlike the experiences of women with children. Generally, the women I interviewed remained optimistic about family life after release.

6

Ageing in Their Own Words: Peace of Mind, Body, and Circumstances

This chapter considers ageing – in prison and in general – from the perspective of the women I interviewed. The women described ageing as influencing various forms of acceptance.

In fact, the older women I interviewed initiated very little discussion about ageing in prison. Many of them mentioned their age or talked about getting older only when asked a direct question. Several of my prompts directed older participants to consider the influence, if any, age had on their incarceration experience (for example, Would you talk to me about older and younger inmates?). However, only a few of the women *voluntarily* discussed their age as a causal factor in any change in behaviour or perspective. They more often attributed their reform to the adoption or strengthening of religious belief. Fourteen of the women I interviewed mentioned religiosity or spirituality. Anna, who was 53 and in prison for the third time, referred to God 22 times. While most of my participants, like Anna, relegated earlier indiscretions to the time of their youth, they did not necessarily mark the change as age related.

Kay, serving time for a parole violation, was dubious, saying, "the older, the wiser? I don't know. I'm back at 51."

Whereas older participants did not necessarily talk about wisdom, I was nonetheless struck by their astute methods of coping and surviving behind bars, and the sources of hope they discovered with time. The women's statements about surviving create a more nuanced, and gendered, picture of Clemmer's (1940) 'prisonization' and related studies. What they needed to survive – physical and mental challenges – was striking.

Difficulties associated with physical health

The older women in this study reported a multitude of ailments such as high blood pressure, diabetes, lupus, and rheumatoid arthritis, to name only a few. For example, Jane, aged 55, stated that she suffered from lupus, deteriorating discs, rheumatoid arthritis, and a knee that "gives out on her". She reported, "I don't sleep as well. I need more pillows and the mattress is bad." Dalia is 45 and uses a Zimmer/walking frame. She listed her medical conditions as rheumatoid arthritis, degenerative disc disease in her back, heel spurs on both feet, heart disease, nerve damage, borderline diabetes, and hypertension. She has had multiple hip and back surgeries, and knee replacements. She told me that she is taking medicine for all of these conditions. I asked Dalia how she fares behind prison walls, and she replied:

> 'I have good days and bad days. Even on bad days I try to get up and do what I can. I have a job here. It makes me feel good about myself. I work in the supply closet. I try to stay busy to make time pass. Sometimes, my difficulty depends on the temperature or how long I sit or stand. I have a note for early food and medicine.'

Betty, a 43-year-old White woman and a long-termer, said that she took 'chemo' medications for rheumatoid arthritis and required other medications for an autoimmune disease in order to keep walking. Indeed, 12 of the 29 women I interviewed suffered from rheumatoid arthritis and all of them described rheumatoid arthritis as a debilitating disease that affected their daily functioning. (Betty said, "I have good days and bad.") The physical limitations caused by even minor health conditions or natural deterioration of muscle and organ functioning can affect daily life. Several women, for example, complained that their joints hurt more in colder weather.

People requiring wheelchairs often rely on others to push them around on campus. The help may or may not be forthcoming. Jane, 55, observed, "When the women in wheelchairs want to be pushed to medical, the younger women just keep walking." On the other hand, Doris, 62, who used a wheelchair, reported that the younger residents in her dorm were quick to help her get around campus. Mable, 53, who also required a wheelchair, told me that her disability is her greatest difficulty, saying, "The doctor does not want me to push myself, but I don't want to ask for help. My hand swells when I push myself."

All three women in my sample who required the use of a wheelchair reported some difficulty in navigating the prison campus, whether it was related to building access, the location of their dorm on a steep hill, or difficulty in securing assistance from others. Physical handicaps and routine daily activities can be a challenge in a setting that cultivates little sympathy for others' ailments.

Encountering disrespect and a lack of compassion

Perceptions of how incarcerated people are treated by staff bear mentioning because, in a society that preaches respecting one's elders, my participants were particularly cognizant of being viewed first and foremost as inmates. Eleven of my research participants discussed the notion of respect – what they gave and what they received, especially where prison staff were concerned. While I did not ask about prison staff or treatment, my participants commented on the overall lack of compassion for the people in prison, particularly for the older women. Clara, 65, said that she refers to guards and prison administrators much younger than she is as 'sir' or 'ma'am' out of respect for their position of authority. Yet, Clara later mentioned the lack of respect from the officers for those who are incarcerated. She said despite her failing health, she was still expected to work and that she knew of one person with muscular sclerosis who was fired from her janitorial job because she could not stand up to clean. Anna, 53, similarly reported a discussion she had overheard between a guard and someone who was also incarcerated, "A guard told one woman, who was 69, that her bunk was on top. She said, 'I can't get up there.' The guard said, 'You should have thought of that when you got charged.'"

The two most prevalent areas of mistreatment for my research participants were the distribution of medicines and medical services. At Pewee Valley, the residents are required to stand in line to receive their medicines, referred to as the 'Medline.' Six of my participants complained, unprompted, about the Medline being located outside. Frances, 53, stated, "It is cold. They give us thin coats. We have to buy toboggans [hat] and gloves. The Medline is out in the weather, but the officers have a canopy. They don't care because we're prisoners."

A few of the women reported 'doing without' some medications to avoid having to stand in line to get them. Mary, 54, does not take pain relievers because her joints hurt more when it is cold outside; standing in line does her more harm than good. In general, my participants did not understand why they were not allowed shelter from the elements. Anna said, "You have to stand out in the rain. They write you up if you don't get your medicine. There is room for us inside. Why can't we get inside?" The women often described their experiences with Medline as somewhat degrading. Betty referred to it as "cruel and unusual punishment." Similarly, several of my research participants volunteered comments about the prison medical services.

Generally, they cited long waits for services and insufficient diagnosis and treatment. In one extreme case, more of a commentary on prison staff rather than medical staff per se, Joy reported a pregnant person actually giving birth before receiving any attention from staff. Many of my participants blamed what they perceived as inadequate services on a lack of compassion by prison staff. Yet, not all of my participants shared the same disdain and resentment for the available medical services. Three of the participants said they were pleased with the medical doctor and staff. Doris praised them. She said,

"They have a great medical staff. They take care of all my needs. I have to wait to see them, but good once I get in." I cannot speak with certainty of these dichotomous opinions regarding prison health care, but during my interviews, I gleaned from some of my participants that their health services prior to incarceration were poor or non-existent. I therefore assume that prison offered them services they would not normally receive, and they had no real basis for comparison. Overall, my participants required fairly regular medical visits and services – generally familiarizing them with the health care system more than younger people, as my three younger participants made no specific mention of their experiences with the medical staff.

Shame of ageing in prison

Incarceration not only takes a physical toll on older people in prison but has a psychological effect as well. Previous research has established that the abusive and traumatic backgrounds of most incarcerated women generally result in serious depression and post-traumatic stress disorder (Farley and Kelly, 2000; Marcus-Mendoza and Wright, 2003). Suh (2000) found that incarceration exacerbates existing mental illness. In fact, nearly two thirds of my participants had received some mental diagnosis ranging from mild depression to schizophrenia. Yet, I also observed a more profound emotional response among my older participants. As previously mentioned, my participants did not readily initiate any discussion regarding their age, but they would respond to direct questions regarding the same. Thus, I began to realize that their age was actually a source of shame. Frances, 53, who has served four years of a 12-year sentence, shared, "I used to be very vain. I'm going through menopause. I've changed physically and mentally. Sometimes I try to pretend I'm not in prison. I never thought I would ever be in prison. I'm sad that I'm doing my old age in here."

At least five of my research participants specifically referred to ageing in prison as embarrassing.

Gina: Talk to me about ageing in prison.
Margaret: I'm ashamed of being here at my age.
Gina: Why?
Margaret: I don't know why I feel that way, but I do. ... I'll carry the shame for a while.

Feelings of embarrassment and shame are social: they involve the perception of evaluation by external observers. Thus, I assume the women I spoke with perceived themselves to have failed to meet social expectations associated with older adults, including those of the senior being virtuous, wise, and at leisure. Mary, who was in prison for the second time, admitted "Growing old in jail is demeaning. ... Old lady in jail. I should know better than to be here." For the most part, the older women I interviewed indicated that they had accepted ageing as they had accepted their incarceration.

It bears mentioning that my older participants were by and large respected by younger ones because of their age. Generally regarded as 'old-timers', older people who are incarcerated are often admired for their ability to 'do their time'. Misty, a 50-year-old long-termer, was one of several of the older women I spoke with who talked about her respected status among the others. She said, "They call me Miss Misty. That makes me feel good." In this way, age, which is a source of shame in the eyes of free society, becomes a source of pride within the prison. Nevertheless, most of my older participants were cognizant that they were not 'living up' to social expectations by being an 'old-timer' rather than a productive member of society. Thus, as older people in prison, they admitted to lamenting wasted years and regretting their past behaviours. Many of my participants stated they felt ashamed of past actions, generally in the context of their children as discussed in the previous chapter, but several of them also discussed behaviours that they are now embarrassed to recall. Sue, a long-termer, shared, "I'm upset about why I acted like I did when I first got here." Sue admitted she was reckless and engaged in deviant activity upon first entering prison years ago. Other participants recalled their criminal behaviours prior to their incarceration with a fair amount of disdain and embarrassment. Mary, a short-termer, recalled, "I would ride around in my car and ask for money. I would tell them I needed gas. I made money for two to three years. I would get mad if I didn't get anything. They didn't owe me anything. It's embarrassing to me now." Mary, in particular, spoke at length about her indiscretions as a professional panhandler to support her drug addiction. On more than one occasion she laughed as she recalled what she referred to as her 'ridiculous behaviour'. Mary, like several of my other older participants, had acceptance, but lingering embarrassment regarding her past.

Three types of acceptance

Persons entering prison experience a period of adjustment, or what has been referred to as *adaptation* to the new environment. While all people who are incarcerated go through a similar adaptation process, not all of them will experience every aspect of it. Rose Giallombardo (1966) and David Ward and Gene Kassebaum (1965) argue in two early studies of homosexuality among women in prison that such behaviour was the major mode of adaptation to the prison environment. Other studies reveal pseudo-families as a means of adaptation (Mahan, 1984). Adaptation is thought to happen rather quickly as one must immediately 'learn the ropes' in order to survive. Acceptance, on the other hand, proved to be a much more difficult hurdle for many of my research participants. Acceptance, like life itself, is a journey that takes time, presumably years, to achieve. For the older women in my sample, acceptance occurred on three levels: acceptance of incarceration, acceptance of responsibility, and acceptance of self. Many of the women I interviewed indicated that while they did not like being in prison, they *accepted* it. Acceptance should not be considered equivalent to complacency, contentment, or a sense of comfort. I define acceptance as the act of resolving oneself to the inability to change one's current circumstances and the decision to make the most of it. In this section, I explore the nature of acceptance as expressed by my participants.

Acceptance of incarceration

Most of the women I spoke with had accepted their stay in prison, but the manner or degree of acceptance varied based on sentence length and time served. For the women I spoke with, the key difference was that short-termers have a release date; that is, they know when they are leaving. Polly, 44, must serve at least three years of her 15-year sentence for assault (shaking) of her infant step-grandchild before her first parole hearing. She stated, "The hardest thing to have in here is hope of getting out, unless you have an out date." The long-termers had to accept their incarceration and the possibility that they might never be released. The short-termers, on the other hand, accepted prison as a temporary circumstance – presumably a much easier reality to accept. While my younger participants also had accepted their incarceration, the youngest of my participants was 27 years old. According to the women I spoke with, the people who tend to have a more difficult time dealing with their incarceration are younger still. Thus, I cannot offer more than the accounts given to me by my participants for a comparison between acceptance among older and younger people who are incarcerated.

Acceptance of incarceration for older short-termers, who entered prison middle aged or older, happened relatively quickly compared to long-termers. All of the long-termers had 'grown up' behind bars and mentioned some type of behavioural and emotional transformation from when they first entered prison. Generally, the transformation took many years, in some cases more than 15, to complete, but, in the end, all of the older long-termers had accepted their incarceration. Betty, 43, has served 12 years of a life sentence.

Gina: Is there any difference between you then and now?
Betty: When I came to prison, I was a bitch. I would fight over everything. I just wanted people to respect me. I had to learn to change my attitude. You took everything away from me. I'm not here to be happy about that. But, I have to accept it. That's reality. I thought if I accept it, they win. I changed that (thought).

Eve, 51, has served seven years of a life sentence. She described her initial period of denial upon first entering prison. "I was real depressed. I went to Medline and took so much medicine that I slept till the next day – I was very withdrawn – I didn't want to have to deal with nothing. I did that for about a year." Eve reported that she "grew up" after four years.

Gina: What do you mean 'grew up'?
Eve: I realized if I could do it again, I would do it different. I've been high my whole life. This is the first time I've been clean. After four years, I grew up – see things in a grown up way.

In fact, like Betty and Eve, all of the long-termers I interviewed reported some initial stage of rebellion and denial followed by their current stage of acceptance. Sue, who has served 21½ years, said, "I'm okay. I'm pretty happy." Generally speaking, the moment of acceptance came when the women, long-termers in this instance, experienced a change of mindset, what might even be called an epiphany. At some point they had made a choice; they *chose* to use their 'time' in order to improve themselves. A common mantra among the women was 'Don't let prison do *you*, you do prison.' And so, for whatever reason, the women reported a decision to make the most out of the time they had, such as furthering their education or enrolling in self-help classes. Rose, serving 13 years for manslaughter, commented several times on the opportunities afforded to people in prison.

Gina: What is it like here?
Rose: They've got a lot of activity here. It is like a college. Either you learn or you don't learn. I consider myself as learned. I'm further in my mind than I was. You can get a GED and college degree in here.

Nearly all of my older research participants reported participating in prison programmes and educational opportunities. Kay, a 52-year-old short-termer, has served 15 months. She stated, "You can better yourself here. I'm working on my GED. There is lots to do here. You either have to apply yourself, or you can do dead time." All eight of the long-termers in my sample had participated in self-help and educational classes. Evelyn, who has served 12 years of a life sentence, offered the best example of taking advantage of prison time for self-improvement.

Gina: Is there any difference between you then and now?
Evelyn: Everyone knew me as 'she-devil', now I'm learned. I wanted to have a chance to get back out so people could see me in a different light.

Gina: Why?

Evelyn: The older you get, you begin to face the reality that you are going to die. You get a whole new perspective. Some women sit home for years and do nothing. I'm amazed at myself and what I've done.

Gina: Like what?

Evelyn: I have gotten over 400 certificates, diplomas, and degrees. I did everything you could in here.

Evelyn, like others in my sample and especially long-termers, discussed her quest to stay busy as an essential part of her 'new perspective' and reform.

Betty, a long-termer who had recently received a 10-year deferment, stated, "I've taken every self-help class here. I have ten more years now. What am I going to do with it? Time gets very boring. Health goes down and start mentally losing it. I've seen it." For long-termers, inactivity equalled 'dead time' – a scary prospect for women facing long sentences.

Acceptance of responsibility

Most of the older research participants expressed a critical stance on their behaviours and the effects thereof. Relatedly, they accepted responsibility for their own incarceration. Jane observed, "Some inmates get $100 a week. If they don't, they call someone and chew them out. I say be thankful for what you got. They [your family] didn't put you here." The older people judged themselves and others. May said, "I regret selling drugs again – should have left it alone. If I had I wouldn't be here today." Frances observed, "The person on [the] outside no longer exists. I take my responsibility. I hurt a lot of people." Sue, a long-termer, said that accepting blame took time. "Taken all this for me to get in touch with myself. I didn't set out to do it, but I was a part of that crime." A sense of responsibility brought some feelings of shame and guilt. Most of the older women I spoke with reported that they had accepted responsibility, dealt with their shame and guilt, and eventually learned to like themselves. I note that two of my participants, in effect, denied responsibility for their incarceration. Clara stated that all of the allegations were fictitious and that no crimes were committed. For Clara, the court system had failed to deliver justice. Betty denied any wrongdoing; thus, for her, she has no crime to take responsibility for committing.

Nevertheless, my older participants, while they openly disclosed histories of child abuse, domestic abuse, alcohol and drug addiction, and other external factors that were prevalent at the time their crimes were committed, they still admitted that they did it. Acceptance of responsibility, for most of my participants, was the first step in initiating their reform or change of mindset. Is acceptance of responsibility necessary for reform? Clara and

Betty have both been incarcerated for over ten years. During that time, Clara has accumulated two associate degrees, a paralegal diploma, and nine credits towards a bachelor's degree. Betty has taken various self-help classes and "strengthened her relationship with God". Therefore, I do not view acceptance of responsibility as a necessary predecessor to reform. However, my participants' acceptance of responsibility was remarkable to me because the majority of them would have reason to disavow themselves of responsibility for their crimes due to issues of abuse and/or drug addiction. Yet, none of my participants claimed to be a victim. For them, everything they had experienced, in some way, made them stronger. Thus, they were able to admit that they committed the crime, had accepted responsibility for their incarceration, and; furthermore, most of them reported they had forgiven themselves.

Acceptance of self

Older participants talked about two selves: the self then and the self now. Long-termers frequently talked about their behaviours as young people first entering prison. Misty, who has served 23 years of a life sentence, recalled, "When I first came in, I was still involved in drugs. ... I was bitter, because of everyone I hurt. ... Anything illegal, I was involved in – right there in the middle of it." But Misty continued, "A lot goes on in prison. I've changed, gotten older, getting more spiritual. I want change; I want something different for my family." Elle, a 51-year-old long-termer, recalled:

> 'I used to be so angry. Look at me wrong, I'd take your head off. The bastard I was with made me an evil person. If you go after me, I'm going to get you back. If God intended for any of us to be abused, man would be born with a club and you born as punching bag. No one should be in that kind of situation. After all that abuse, he made me become an abuser. I became over-defensive. I regretted that.'

Today, Elle said she smiles at everybody and cooks for the 'girls' in her dorm. Long-termers said that age and maturity have transformed them from who they were 'then' to who they are now.

Almost all of the older participants reported that they liked themselves and, for many, it was for the first time. Kay said, "I've worked on myself more this time than I ever have. I love myself today and who I can be. I've never done that before. I always thought I wasn't worth it." Self-discovery was, it seemed, a process via which incarcerated people learn to accept themselves. In other words, age was important because it was sometimes necessary to survive the bad and come out on 'the other side' in order to truly appreciate one's strength and strengths. June, a short-termer who almost died from the horrific abuse by her ex-husband, recalled what her mother, who had survived breast cancer, had once told her: "We are survivors. We are made of strong stuff and you never forget that." She added, "I will survive." Mable, another short-termer, found her self-confidence during her incarceration. She stated, "I'm a lot stronger. I discovered strength I didn't know I had – I feel like I can go back out in society and make decisions I never could before. I've learned things here. ... I like myself now. I didn't always." While all of my older participants reported liking themselves, none of my younger participants declared the same. At the same time, they did not confess to not liking themselves, but it was my impression that it was something they were still working on at the time. Older people are privy to hindsight, foresight, and experience; thus, they are capable of achieving acceptance on several levels.

The young according to the old

Whatever else it is, incarceration is forced interaction. Consequently, one's prison experience is affected, in one way or another, by other incarcerated people. For the older women in this study, the prison experience was affected by their relationship with younger women. Two behavioural habits were consistent among all of the older participants in the study. First, older people avoided the dayroom because of the noise, drama, and fighting of the rebellious younger women, preferring the comparative quiet and solitude of their own rooms. Second, they reported not associating or 'hanging out' with the immature and troublesome young people, opting instead to be alone or seek company with others their age or, on occasion, with the sensible younger individuals who may ask them for advice.

Some younger participants were recognized for showing respect to the older ones and even voluntarily assisting the women in wheelchairs. Doris was a 62-year-old short-termer who suffered from several physical ailments. She stated, "Where I'm living, those girls are great. I didn't feel good yesterday – all of them asked if I needed anything." Mary, incarcerated multiple times, observed, "Girls here respect you for being older. Call me Miss Mary. That makes me feel good." On the other hand, Clara, a long-termer, considered younger residents to be "crooked as hell and getting worse." Perspective, whether one is in prison or free society, comes with age, including perspective on how the behaviour of others is not unlike one's past behaviour. Similar to an elderly lady shaking her fist and upbraiding 'those darn kids', older people are in a position, albeit involuntary, to observe the repeated mistakes and rare triumphs of the younger generation.

According to my older research participants, the younger women who are commonly serving short sentences do not take incarceration seriously and typically receive more than adequate financial support from their families during their term. Carol stated, "They don't take it seriously. It is like a vacation – let them out and six months or six weeks later they're back." The problem, according to Christy, is that "young girls are getting $100 per month and spending it all while others are making state pay – $8 per month." She mused, "The young aren't learning hardships."

Many of my participants were angered by observing the younger women choose drugs over their children because they are aware of the consequences over time. Evelyn, a long-termer observed, "The young ones want to make contraband headbands, but what about a blanket for your baby or mother?" Dalia stated, "The young have a hard life, but we all do. They would rather write men in prison than family. I don't understand that. It makes me angry, as a matter of fact." Older participants said that they would relish the chance at freedom; they see younger women throwing that chance away again and again. Stella reported: "In here ain't nothing to them. They think it is a joke. Get out and do the same shit all over again. I got a chance to get out – that's it – I'm not looking to come back."

Stella continued, "[They] act like it's nothing. I don't understand it. They act like their shit don't stink. They say they'll do the same stuff again. You'd never see me again."

The younger women are generally regarded as the children of the residents. They are 'babies having babies'. Older women, especially long-termers, are particularly sensitive to and often irritated by their presence. My participants believed that younger women did not care or, perhaps, they were too young to care. Frances observed:

'Older inmates show respect to other inmates and staff. They follow rules. Just try to do their time. Young girls don't wear uniforms correctly. No respect for officers or elders. They just don't care. "I'm just here for this time. You're a lifer. You can go to hell." Officers know young ones are out of line when they say things like this.'

Dalia remarked, "They think this is a game. ... You shouldn't do that. They want you to be productive in here. Young ones don't want to be. They are very disrespectful, rude, and angry." Whereas the older research participants said that younger women frequently ask family members for money and also write to men on the outside – 'tricks' – and ask for money. These older women said that they were generally less concerned about money. They had learned to stretch their state pay from their prison job and accepted state-issued shoes and other paid-for amenities. Jane reported, "Young ones want name brand names. A lot of them have not grown up. I had to take care of my kids. They think everyone should take care of them." Kay observed, "A lot of younger ones have to have name brand shoes – $60/$70 shoes – have to have best of the best. But in prison, who's going to see your shoes?" With reportedly few exceptions, older women described their younger counterparts as materialistic and self-centred. They reported that younger women formed close relationships with others in order to gain material items such as food and clothing. Dalia reported that she had to learn to not be as trusting, particularly with the younger participants. "I'm family-oriented. Sometimes I get hurt here. I believe in friendship. Inmates are very manipulative. My roommate – saw her as my child. She stole my clothes when she left (to go to another prison). It hurt. I cried." Jane said, "Young inmates only think about themselves and taking care of their woman, or latch on to someone who will take care of them."

Thus, lesbian relationships were said to be a playground for many of the younger women. Margaret, who reported being a lesbian for a long time, stated, "To most of the girls it's a game. Some kind of emotional game they play." Younger women were accused of using other residents for financial support and simply as a way to pass the time. Dalia, 45, observed, "They want attention and love. It is not real love. They do it to get what they want – might have two per cent gay on the street – rest have never been with a woman before but do in here."

Despite these negative evaluations of the young women, except for one older long-termer, the older women in this study reported that they had had no major altercations with their younger counterparts. For the most part, the older women reported ignoring the behaviours of the younger ones. They would only get involved if the behaviours became overtly disrespectful. Jane recalled an incident when two younger women were 'flaunting' their relationship. "I've been called a rat before – two women in the bathroom where everyone could see and I told – I found it disrespectful to me."

Thus, on a day-to-day basis, younger and older women in prison are able to live together in reasonable harmony. According to my research participants, age and maturity provide older women with some level of implicit hierarchical authority. While not all of the younger women acknowledge or respect this authority, the older ones generally keep the peace. All of the older women I interviewed reported that older women support each other and act as a cohesive group. Betty, a long-termer, stated, "Long-timers won't put up with the young inmates. ... Young ones think they can throw us over, but they learn fast." Clara, another long-termer who had served 18 years of a life sentence, declared:

> 'Before, if an officer said something to the girls, they would stop what they were doing. Now, they rebel. Why rebel? That's a big question. ... We're getting a crosscut of society. Much more crooked and rebellious. More self-centered. They don't care. We don't have law and order. Too much turnover. [They all] treat me the same. They know I won't take

it. I tell on them in front of someone else. I tell them if I'm reporting it, don't like it, but I'm not sneaky.'

Older women in prison reportedly spend much of their time alone. When they do socialize, older women generally reported seeking companions close to their own age or length of sentence.

Relationships among older women in prison

While the older women frequently reported spending time in their rooms and keeping to themselves, it was not unusual for them to also mention significant relationships with others their own age. While some of my participants were homosexual, the women who discussed their relationships with other women reportedly sought a deep emotional connection with another person. Several of the older participants who reported engaging in these relationships were gay or bisexual prior to their incarceration. Therefore, their behaviours were generally a continuation of their lives in free society. Older participants who did not report participating in lesbian relationships were by and large very understanding and accepting of those who did. Furthermore, all of the older research participants mentioned relationships involving prison moms and prison daughters, whether or not they ever participated in these relationships themselves. Due to the caring and nurturing nature of these relationships, I will explore them in greater detail in the next chapter dealing with generativity. While not all of the older women engaged in these relationships, they were very important to those who did. Therefore, this section will briefly explore the nature of those relationships among older women in prison.

I return to the previous discussion regarding younger people who are incarcerated because my participants appeared particularly bothered or angered by the carelessness with which younger people treated other women's emotions. All of the older lesbians harboured some disdain for younger women whom they referred to as 'gay for the stay'. Margaret stated, "I'm a lesbian – have been for a long time. If I do get with somebody, I keep it respectful – not for sex. I tell them [younger inmates] that they make us 'fucking faggots' look bad." In fact, all of the older women who took part in lesbian relationships specified that their relationships were based on companionship and not sex. It seemed to some extent that the older women were deterred from more intimate contact by current prison regulations. Many of the older participants, particularly long-termers, had 'honours', which entitled them to a private room and access to a stove for cooking. In order to keep their honours they had to maintain 'good behaviour'; sexual contact with another woman in prison would result in the loss of their honour privileges. Others reported that all they desired was to have someone with whom they could talk and share a close bond. It was not uncommon for older women to seek a close companion.

Betty, serving a life sentence, said:

> 'I have a girlfriend. Everybody thinks it's all about sex. We need affection, companionship. A lonely woman is like a scorned woman. We're made to be loved. I love men, but in here, it's another world – whole new world. Gotta do what I gotta do for me. They should let us do what we want. Lots of people hold their girlfriend's hand. There's nothing nasty about it. It's not hurting nobody. What is the sense in hiding it?'

Eve, another long-termer, stated, "As much time as I have – I seek a companion, but not sexually. I haven't found that companion."

While older women estimated homosexual activity to be quite high (80 per cent or higher), their estimates of 'true' lesbian relationships were very low (mostly two to five per cent). By and large, lesbian relationships were viewed as manipulative, either for attention or material gain and simply as a way to pass the time for many younger residents. Several long-termers admitted to 'hustlin'', or engaging in relationships for material gain, within prison, when they were younger, but reported that they did not do it anymore. Again, like other wild behaviours of their youth, older women had aged out of what they now consider to be wrongful behaviour. They often cited that they were tired of 'the game', which is primarily played by the younger women, and are now more content with being by themselves. Misty, a long-termer, admitted:

> 'My relationships were mostly based on companionship. ... I used to write pen pals or get girlfriends – Oriental, Black – whatever I wanted, I got it, but everything was for a game. It made me feel good about myself. I thought it made me look good. People said, "Misty takes care of her women." Then, I woke up and thought, "This game is all wrong." I've been more content ever since.'

Misty reported that she realized her relationships were for show and not about any real emotions. She no longer participates in homosexual relationships and claims to much be happier.

Whereas I detected no homophobia, older women framed sexual relationships in prison as sites of manipulation and duplicity.

The women also sought out platonic relationships with fellow prison residents. While earlier research outlined complex interrelations of moms, dads, daughters, cousins, aunts, and more (Giallambardo, 1966), the older women at Pewee Valley referred only to prison moms, daughters, and sisters; all of these were terms for individuals sharing closeness and loyalty. The term 'friend' was used by some of my participants to describe another incarcerated woman, but close friends were also called 'sisters'. Evelyn, a long-termer said, "I have two true friends – long-termers – two lifers."

Older women, particularly long-termers, reported supporting each other as a family unit. Kay observed, "All older inmates respect each other." Betty said, "Long-timers stick together. This is all we have. You become a family in here. My prison 'sister' is about to leave and I cry every day about it. We take care of each other."

Most of the older women found comfort in talking to other incarcerated women. Indeed, some simply found comfort in talking to anyone, as they spoke of the interview as therapeutic.

Older women in prison cope with incarceration

Long-termers in particular reported periods of ups and downs. Several of the long-termers expressed doubt that they would ever leave prison. The older women I interviewed reported that they had to occasionally take their minds off of the unknown, such as if and when they would leave, in order to survive day to day. The difference between older women in prison and their younger counterparts is clearly evident in the way the two groups handle the 'downs'. Frances said, "I have six years to go, but I see I'm fortunate that that is all I have. I have a date I'm leaving. Lifers are going to die in here." Elle stated, "I've learned someone is a little worse off than I am. Some people say I'm mean, (younger inmates) will be bellyaching about four months. I'll say 'suck it up – look at these doing 20 years'."

Polly described a long-termer who recently received a 20-year deferment, time that must be served before the person in prison is eligible for another parole hearing, from the parole board, "[She] has gone through every programme offered, but she had a violent crime, and she really thought she might have a chance. [After deferment] she was really down for a few days but accepted it. She could handle it, but it was harder on her family."

The prison literature led me to wonder about coping among this unique population. Scholars before me have generally focused on younger people in prison and their responses to the loneliness and the deprivations of prison life – namely the formation of pseudo-families and the engagement in homosexual relationships (Mahan, 1984; Morris, 1987). While my participants reported relating to other people in prisons either as associates, friends, sisters, or intimate companions, these relationships were not constant. The two most prevalent and dependable coping mechanisms were religion and themselves.

Having faith

Over half of my participants attributed their ability to cope with incarceration to God and their faith. Religion is not typically mentioned as a way of coping in studies focusing on younger people in prison (Owen, 1998; Girshick, 1999). Likewise, my three younger participants did not mention ideologies of faith or comfort obtained from religious beliefs. Evelyn, who was recently given a 20-year deferment by the parole board, said of getting older in prison:

> '[It's] just one of them things. I will be 60 years old before I can be paroled. I'm getting old – going to die – that goes through my mind, but God is with me. I have to have faith. I stay positive and say I'm going to get out even if I'm in a wheelchair or on oxygen.'

The women also typically credited God with their reform. Elle stated:

> 'Over the years, I have asked God to change me. He brought me change. When I rewind my life, I look at all the stupid things. It is only by grace of God that I didn't die or kill someone else. When a lot of people don't like you because of who you became, you have to humble yourself.'

In many ways, my participants reported finding the most comfort in their faith. They regarded religion as something constant in their lives, thus God would be with them during the duration of their incarceration.

Time for self

The day-to-day routines of the women I spoke with were centred around *their* work assignments and *their* free time. The women asserted their independence, as much as the prison allowed. Imprisonment occasioned meditation on the self and care of the body. Quiet, self-facing time alone was valued.

All of the older women reported trying to stay busy in order to help pass the time. Elle, a 51-year-old serving time for manslaughter, stated:

> 'I use time constructively. I take my mind out of this place. My mind is in the street. I'm in my own zone. I made a book – what I wanted my life to be. What I wanted surrounding me. It had a house and other things. I'm in the middle of it. On my bulletin board, I have a collage with a variety of things. Picture of bedroom suite, sexy, fine men, cans of food. Nice things in life. I always want to be surrounded by people.'

For many, physical exercise was a common way to fill free time. Rose, or 'Granny', stated, "If you keep exercising and eating proper and doing what they tell you, you won't age as fast. But, if you sit around and worry a lot about being in prison, you will age faster." Pewee Valley offers a recreation programme specifically for women at least 42 years of age – generally designed with the needs and limitations of this age group in mind. While two of the women in my sample mentioned participating in that particular programme, at least half reported getting regular exercise on their own. Sue stated, "I exercise a lot. I encourage other older women to exercise. I want to live to walk out of here." Stella is a 52-year-old short-termer who takes care of herself in this way:

Gina: Tell me about life for you here.
Stella: At 52, I'm having a hard time anyway. Now just passing days until I get out of here. I exercise: stair stepping, treadmill, weights – try to keep sugar down.

Stella's attempts to manage diabetes with exercise raised a point about the prison diet. I wondered if prison fare was a problem. A few of the women I interviewed mentioned specific dietary needs that were hard to accommodate in prison. For example, Jane, 55, had an iron deficiency, but she was able to buy beans from the commissary to supplement meals in the cafeteria. The women did not typically complain about the food that was available and seemed to be able to adapt their diet accordingly.

Passing time was also a mental exercise and a solitary one. Frances, a 53-year-old first-timer, reported, "Sometimes I try to pretend I'm not in prison." My participants also reported spending a significant amount of time by themselves. Clara, who has served 18 years of a life sentence, said, "I sit at a cold table in the lunchroom, so no one will sit with me." Sally said, "I don't go out in dayroom. I stay hibernated in my room. People try to get me out of there." Indeed, for many of my participants, being alone was preferable to the noise of others and often gave them time to do things which they enjoyed, such as reading or crocheting.

I can see clearly now, my freedom's gone

The experience of incarceration was heavily influenced by health issues that coincided with getting older, as well as their ability to accept aspects of their lives that they might have denied when they were younger. The women in my sample reported numerous physical ailments often affecting their daily routine and entailing special needs – which they accepted as part of the natural process of ageing. The psychological effect of being an older prison resident included, for some, shame and embarrassment.

Yet, all of the older research participants reported what I term three levels of acceptance. They learned to accept: (1) their incarceration, (2) responsibility for their crime, and (3) themselves. Acceptance seemed to be a journey aided by age and maturity. Acceptance of incarceration eased the passing of time and often led to peace of mind. Acceptance of responsibility, perhaps the first step to achieving generativity, was fairly universal, remarkable because many of their lives were characterized by victimization more than by offending behaviour. Finally, acceptance of self, which may be the most difficult kind of acceptance, allowed many of the women to feel good about themselves for the first time.

Acceptance of self was the only type of acceptance not shared by my younger participants. Whereas older research participants spoke of liking themselves – many for the first time in their lives – such was not the case for the three participants under age 40. Generally, acceptance of self is tied to being able to forgive oneself for past mistakes, and my younger participants had not yet been able to do so. Acceptance on any level influences the ability to navigate the prison environment and deal with the realities of incarceration.

7

'Usefulness' of a 'Useless' Population

Generative adults hope that the lives of their children and future generations generally will be good and will hold meaning and value. They seek to care for and positively contribute to society and the people they leave behind. The model of generativity presented by Erik Erikson (1950) and elaborated upon by Dan McAdams and Ed de St Aubin (1992) assumes that individuals want to care for future generations because they were cared for by others. I contend that the theory of generativity assumes that an individual lives in free society. By general definition, at least in the Western justice system, a person who is incarcerated has been convicted of a crime against society; people in prison are furthermore thought of as moral transgressors. The notion of generative desires and behaviours among a population of transgressors who have been ostracized by free society would seem an anomaly. However, all 27 of the older women in my study expressed generative thoughts and desires or reported engaging in generative behaviours. The three younger participants did not initiate a discussion of generative thoughts and behaviours. Furthermore, when I prompted them with questions related to generativity, they responded that they do not think about their legacy or what they will leave behind. While one interviewee said that she talked to younger women in prison, she also admitted that she generally tried to avoid it. Nonetheless, I was able to discern thoughts and actions related to generativity, and this chapter shares these. First, I expound upon the concept of generativity.

Erikson introduced the concept of generativity more than 50 years ago. Since that time, researchers have expanded on and departed from certain of his ideas (for example, Browning, 1975; Kotre, 1984; McAdams, 1985; McAdams and de St Aubin, 1992). Generativity has evolved to encompass several principles and behaviours, such as teaching, mentoring, and encouraging the next generation. Due to the nature of incarceration and the 'typical' characteristics of the women who are housed there, it would seem likely that incarcerated people do not express generativity in the same manner or to the same degree as adults outside of prison. For the purpose of this study, I strip the definition of generativity down to the most basic elements first outlined by Erikson (1950). Erikson defined generativity as a commitment to the larger society and its continuation and/or improvement through the next generation (1950). Erikson considered teaching, writing, invention, the arts and sciences, social activism, and generally contributing to the welfare of future generations, all to comprise generativity. Generative adults want to feel needed and ponder the legacy they will leave behind. While Erikson believed the bearing and raising of children were keys to becoming a generative adult – in part due to easy access to the next generation through one's own children – he later conceded that generativity was possible even for those who do not rear children. With these ideas in mind, I identified some elements of generativity articulated by virtually all of my participants.

The study was exploratory and inductive, and as such, my interviewing protocol did not adhere to Erikson's or any other theoretical model. The topic of generativity was of great, early interest to me, yet I allowed the research participants to initiate mention of desires and behaviours related to generativity. Only later in each interview, if necessary, I drew on prompts to encourage them to elaborate on generativity. Twenty-one of my older participants initiated talk of (some aspect of) generativity; yet, I prompted all of them (29) with more specific questions related to generativity, such as regarding their legacy, how they will be remembered, and feelings of responsibility. Doris, a 62-year-old long-termer, spoke readily of sharing her experiences to help 'younger girls':

Gina: How do you see yourself when you get out?
Doris: I'd like to be able to talk to younger girls about going down the road I've gone. I want to talk about life experiences and prison.
Gina: Do you feel a responsibility to help others?
Doris: Yes. I didn't go through this for nothing.

Here, in response to a rather general question, Doris mentioned her desire to lecture younger girls about the consequences of foolish behaviour – a desire I regard as generative. I followed the general prompt with a more generativity-oriented question regarding responsibility, in an attempt to probe her about why she felt the way she did.

One research question, in particular, seemed to stimulate talk of generativity. Early on I asked my participants whether they considered themselves to be victims or offenders. But after one woman asserted that she was a 'survivor', I changed the question to whether they considered themselves to be victims, survivors, or offenders. The majority of the women I spoke with quite zealously declared they were survivors. My research participants had survived relational abuse, alcohol and drug addiction, and other hardships. The attributes they reportedly tried to instil in younger women were influenced by their life experiences and stories of survival.

The virtues of the generative person who is incarcerated are, then, likely to be skills and tools necessary for survival – both of prison life and life hardships. Frances, a short-termer, declared, "I feel like I should pass on what I know. I survived my abusive relationship. I learned a lot. I survived this." The women I spoke with most commonly emphasized the virtuous qualities of patience, hope, and love.

Within the confines of prison, opportunities to directly give back to free society were (and generally are) extremely limited, but opportunities to give to others are comparatively abundant. The women in my sample desired to help others and many of them reported doing so on a daily basis. Sharing food and advising younger women were the two most common examples of helping others. Women shared food and other supplies with others who had less. They also reported advising, tutoring, and sharing their wisdom with the younger women – often giving the older women a sense of being needed. All of the older participants reported encouraging younger women to make better choices. Sometimes the women were 'prison moms' to several younger ones, taking on an explicit and steady maternal role by supporting and looking after their prison daughters. Moreover, upon their release, the women expressed desires to continue to help others, particularly youth, and to 'repay' society for what they had done. While prison regulations and programming may either encourage or inhibit generativity, the women seemed steadfast in their efforts of benevolence. Participants also talked about how they thought they will be remembered and what, if any, legacy they would leave behind. This chapter is about generative behaviours among a group of people whom we generally least expect to care for others.

Younger women in prison as the future generation

All of the older women in my sample reported talking to, listening to, and advising younger women to varying degrees. Of course, such interaction does not make all of the women generative. In fact, sporadic or frequent conversations may simply be the product of forced interaction or boredom and may not contain any generative substance at all. However, when generativity does occur, both participants and general society stand to benefit.

The wish to help younger women in prison was generally expressed in terms of giving to others what they had not had. This pattern leads me to revisit the assumption that an individual wants to care for future generations because they were cared for by others. Amid the many stories of abuse, neglect, and abandonment, I could not reconcile this assumption with the experiences of the older women in my sample. I suggest that generative people in prison want to care for others, namely younger people in prison – their most readily accessible members of future generations – because they themselves were *not* cared for by others. The attitude and reckless behaviours of the younger women reminded the older women I spoke with of themselves as young adults. For example, Mary, 54, a short-termer, recalled her lack of guidance as an adolescent:

> 'When my mom died, my dad didn't tell me nothing – no advice. My sister didn't tell me nothing. I haven't been around anybody to teach me about stuff – to give me direction. I think he (my father) knew about me using drugs, but never said anything.'

Similarly, Elle, a (51-year-old) long-termer, lamented never having what she referred to as a 'strong family'. She stated, "I never had strong family support to tell me I could do things." Like several other research participants, Elle reported a lack of encouragement as a youth. Since the younger women act in ways that my older participants associate with their own youth, the older women surmise that the younger ones have also lacked care and encouragement.

By caring for others, generative adults in free society continue a pattern set by example by those who cared for them. The women I spoke with, on the other hand, lacked examples of generativity but recognized their importance. Anna, 53, observed, "A lot of these girls don't have mothers or family. Growing older is hard. They need someone to say 'I want you to be somebody'." Betty, a 43-year-old long-termer, had a similar feeling:

> 'My God provides for me and tells me what to tell these kids. I've gotten kids in church and turning their life around and in college. I've pushed them because nobody pushed me.'

For my research participants, the desire to care for and encourage younger women in prison does not continue a positive pattern but is an attempt to correct a negative one. In other words, the older women I spoke with recognized the consequences of their not receiving care and encouragement from others and sought to provide both of these things to younger women in an attempt to prevent them from continuing down the same path. Thus, motivations for generativity among the older women in my sample were notably different than that which is assumed for generative adults in free society. Next, I explore the behavioural expression of generative desires among the older women and their ways of fulfilling such desires, in relative order of the frequency with which my research participants reported these.

Listening, advising, and mentoring

While my research participants complained about the attitudes and behaviours of their younger prison mates. None of them reported denying the latter of an attentive audience when they wanted to talk. In fact, listening to the troubles of and offering advice to the more youthful participants appeared to be one of the greatest services older women provided. Mary was a short-termer serving time for a drug offence.

Gina: What is your greatest contribution?
Mary: Talking to girls in here. I ask them, 'What are you going to do?' One girl is trying to be different. I asked her, 'What are you going to do? Going to go back to drug using again? Why don't you think about doing something different?' She said she don't want to do drugs, so maybe she will go in a different direction.

The women I interviewed commonly reported, without prompting, that they regularly advised younger women, particularly in regard to taking care of children. The older women had either raised their children or lost the opportunity to do so due to drugs or incarceration. Several women reported being disheartened at the sight of so many young mothers in prison. While they were admittedly frustrated by the misplaced priorities and the all too familiar behaviours of the younger women – whom several called 'babies raising babies' – they also felt a high level of compassion for them as well. Stella, who had given her three children up for adoption, declared, "I want them to wake up and see what they have and how they keep screwing their lives up."

The women I spoke with were able to advise their younger counterparts with some degree of learned authority because they had behaved in similar ways when they were younger. Sue, a long-termer said "I know how I was, so I understand. I let them know that I truly understand." For many of my participants, the younger people triggered an experience of déjà vu. Thwarting younger women from the same fate was an important goal for Kay, a 52-year-old with a 14-year sentence for manufacturing methamphetamine:

'You see yourself in them and I say, "You know what – do you want to be 52 in prison for 14 years? 'Cause if you keep going, you will be." They say, "I'm not." I say, "Yeah you will, if you don't change." That's what I tell younger girls.'

The exchange between older and younger participants was viewed as mutually beneficial. The women I interviewed reported that sharing their experiences with others helped them to learn about themselves and to forgive their own past mistakes. Margaret was grateful for opportunities to share her experiences:

Gina: Would you talk to me about your relationship with younger inmates?

Margaret: How I see it – when they come to me. They are a different generation, but I understand because I was in a rebellious generation. I give advice about what I've done, what I wish I'd done. I don't sugar coat it. I don't act like it (prison) is a big party. But when I was younger, I thought it. They come to me because I don't sugar coat it. ... Just talking in here, I uncover things about me, too. We both benefit.

Mable reported that her primary goal was to convince younger women to take care of their children before it was too late:

'I talk to them about their children as a priority. Nothing is more precious than children. Yet, drugs took over and now they must face the consequences. I see so many who say they'll get children back, but then they're back here. They leave on parole and come back for a dirty urine test, so they're still putting drugs before kids. It is hard to tell them now that they'll regret it.'

Older participants seemed to have a difficult task in warning younger women about future consequences; the younger women were apt to ignore the warnings. Yet, the women I interviewed reported they continued to try. Stella was a short-termer but also a repeat offender.

'All of us try to listen. A lot of us in here – we weren't bad people. For a lot of the older ones, this is their first time being in trouble, but we can still relate to the younger ones. They are younger and starting to get in trouble. The older ones, a lot of us raised kids, some of us didn't. We know how it was for us. Some younger ones listen. Some are hard-assed and not going to listen. They are going nowhere, except in and out these doors. I've seen them leave and come back within 6 months to serve time out or with new charges.'

Certainly, generative adults on the outside must contend with experience-based cautionary tales and advice falling on deaf ears. Yet, generative people in prison have considerably more trouble due to their audience of rebels and misbehaviours. According to Misty, a long-termer, "They [younger inmates] listen, but go out and do the same thing. Selling bodies, doing drugs – takes a piece of you after a while." Many of the younger women in prison do not listen, but for the women I spoke with, just saving one person from returning to prison made their effort worthwhile. Frances, a 53-year-old short-termer, discussed her motivation for talking to the younger women: "If I could help one person, that would be worth it. Life is an experience. If you don't learn from it, then it is lost."

While generative people continue to encourage younger people in prison to abandon their prior lifestyle, they realize that like themselves at a younger age, many of the younger ones do not know how to do anything different.

Peggy, a short-termer, believed that patience and acceptance were keys to easing the anger and frustration often associated with incarceration for younger women. She observed, "[My experience] is a gift. It can make life so much better, if they could accept it. ... One thing you learn in here is patience. You aren't going anywhere." Evelyn, a long-termer, said, "They have trouble dealing with the outside. I tell them they have to do time in here or outside. You can't do both." Over half of the women I spoke with mentioned, to some degree, the importance of acquiring patience and acceptance for prison survival – something the older women had learned and the younger women had not. For example, Peggy observed:

'All these young girls, they want to fight. Get upset when no one answers when they call. I try to give them advice. I can sit there. I have acceptance. If I could just get them to have acceptance, it would be easier to do this time. I tell them time is a healing agent. I've accepted it calmly. Take each day as it comes. I have my goals. I lived through it.'

The older women had acquired patience over the course of many years. They reported trying to impart their 'patience is a virtue' mentality to a not-so-captive audience of younger women who struggled to acknowledge such experienced wisdom just as they struggled to acknowledge hope for the future. Misty, a long-termer, observed a pattern of learned helplessness among the younger residents. She stated, "I talk to inmates all the time. You'd be surprised the number that want better but don't know things." Twenty-four of the women I spoke with reported that they tried to inspire hope by setting an example of survival and prodding younger women to 'straighten up' and not come back to prison. Elle, a long-termer, said that she was well liked by others and postulated that it was partly because she was honest.

Gina: What do you tell the younger inmates?
Elle: That I made it and they can make it, too. I'm grateful if I can reach anybody. Maybe, they will help someone else. I've learned someone is a little worse off than I am. Young girls will be bellyaching about four months. I'll say suck it up and look

at those doing 20 years. You aren't really doing time. You're going to cry for 6 months when you were prostituting and doing drugs. You weren't crying then. They actually thank me. I make sense to them.

The older women seemed to want to create hope in younger women in prison regardless of whether or not they held any for themselves or not. Peggy, a short-termer, was self-deprecating in her talk with younger residents: "I say I'm 52. I got nothing. I don't care about nothing. It shouldn't be that way." Peggy and other women that I interviewed reported trying to prevent younger people from coming back by giving them some hope for their future. Katherine, a short-termer, said, "When they leave, I say remember here and don't come back."

Stella gave her children up for adoption, so she found the failure of the younger generation to nurture their children particularly frustrating. She stated,

> 'Their babies can't see everything, but when they grow up, they're either going to love or hate you. Most have family taking care of their kids. For some the state has them, but they are having other babies to make up for the ones taken away. But doing the same thing (drugs). I say they gotta wake up. Only you can change.'

The majority of the women in my sample reported talking to younger women about taking care of their children and 'doing the right thing'. Raising children is an area that the older participants knew much about. They had either successfully raised their children or they regretted their mistakes which prevented them from doing so. For Elle, nothing was more important than children.

> 'One girl left here. She's 18 now. I know she's drugging again. She has four kids, but lost three to the state. I get angry. God has given you another chance to be with your child and you're out there doing drugs. Those are innocent children. I can't stand the thought that you let something happen to babies. It tears my heart out. I wasn't blessed to have babies. I always just loved on other people's [babies].'

Elle continued:

> 'I tell girls, "Do I ever hear you say, first, when get out, I'll take my babies shopping or to the movies?" I just hear, "go to a motel with my man." Baby should be your first priority. Girls, nowadays, choose a man or drugs over their own child.'

Most of the women I spoke with held a 'do as I say not as I did' attitude concerning child rearing. They reported trying to impress upon the younger women the importance of being with their children because many of the older women in my sample are now left to deal with the consequences. Anna observed, "Women are actually doping and giving up kids. That's crazy. We're losing our own kids to this." The older women stated they did not want either the children of the younger women or the women themselves to suffer as they have.

In some respects, older women within the prison were viewed as matriarchs – a responsibility which they took seriously. Generative people in prison pass on the virtues and lessons they have learned, albeit slightly different than those of generative adults in free society, they are nevertheless committed to the continuation and betterment of society. The bestowment of knowledge on the younger generation becomes, for many of the older women, a labour of love.

Prison mothers and prison daughters

Rose, a 60-year-old long-termer, talked to me about younger women in prison. She stated, "I talk to them and tell them to get help. The young inmates call me 'Granny'. Some act like they want to put their head on my shoulder and just bawl, but they hold it in. You shouldn't hold it in. I did and now I'm here." Generative adults outside of prison hope the lives of their children and the children of others will be good. In this sense, parenting is still considered a major generative outlet. Incarcerated mothers are then at a disadvantage. Separated from their own children, generative women may seek a prison substitute. That is, they assume the role of 'mother' to younger residents. Rose continued, "They are like kids that didn't listen to their parents. But they did not get the right attention from their parents and are lacking love from their families." In this role, the older women are able to teach and mentor the younger ones in order to provide them with the necessary abilities to improve themselves, thus, also contributing to society at large by encouraging them to become productive citizens.

Pseudo-families were once thought to be quite prevalent in women's prisons, involving complex interrelationships of mothers, uncles, brothers, sisters, and cousins. However, the women of Pewee Valley mentioned only two such meaningful relationships: mother/daughter (perhaps grandmother depending on age) and sisterhood. The relationships were mutually supportive. These small, close networks fall in line with research on socioemotional selectivity theory in prison that suggests that older incarcerated people decrease their circle of close relationships, giving greater emotional value to ageing people in prison (Bond, Thompson, and Malloy, 2005). The older women told me that prison mothers and daughters will often share food or other items. Generative people in prison desire the same things for their prison daughters as they do for their own children. In fact, the interaction is quite similar to that between a birth mother and child. Frances talked about her prison daughters: "She don't have a momma and asked if she could call me 'momma.' I said, 'Yeah.' I told her not to do drugs. I correct them about cussing or acting up and they listen. A lot of younger people will turn to older ones who are trying to do right." The women in my sample often reported trying to set an example for the younger women in prison, particularly concerning how to do 'easy time' – that is, stay out of trouble. Most importantly, older participants tried to keep their prison daughters from making the wrong decisions. Carol, a short-termer, stated:

> 'A lot of them call me "Mom". It makes me feel good that they look up to me. It's a respect thing. I listen a lot and try to steer them in the right direction. If they are going to fight, I step in and stop them. I have a maternal interest.'

In addition, the older women I interviewed said they teach and mentor their 'prison daughters' as they would their own children. Betty, a long-termer, reported that younger women respected her status of 'old-timer' and tended to come to her for advice: "Several call me 'Momma' even in their 30s 'cause I'm more mature. I try to help them. They don't understand how I have done the time. I say you have to be strong."

Prison relationships may endure after one person has been released. Stella said, "A couple of them write to me from the outside. A lot are lost because they never really had a mom or grandmom." The older women fill a void for the younger ones who are often searching for a mother figure to guide them. Betty also recalled, "A younger inmate left and said, 'Momma, I will never forget you. You've taught me so much.' It makes me feel real good. I've helped somebody." The older women in my sample, like Betty, truly sought to make a difference for the younger women.

Elle cooked and regularly shared with others who did not have the means to buy for themselves. For her, helping others who were less fortunate was a responsibility.

Gina: Would you talk to me about the younger inmates?
Elle: I'm a mother figure to the younger ones. They call me 'Mamma', but I'm not your mamma. I feed anybody. I get in trouble, but I do it. I encourage young ones to keep them from making wrong decisions. They flock to me … I see young girls in here and try to help them to keep their heads on straight. I've seen it happen. They start with five years, come back in

here, wind up with 15 years. ... They do stupid stuff. I get angry. They say that makes sense when I say something. Lot of them don't have anybody. One inmate said, 'You fuss and remind me of a grandmother. You teach me things I didn't know.' That makes you feel good.

While not all of the women in my sample participated in mother-and-daughter prison relationships, it was mutually beneficial for those who did. The younger women received the nurturing, guidance, and tutelage they were not afforded growing up. The older participants gained a generative outlet through which they were able to inspire others to do better and pass on what they had learned to others, namely to their young children. Of course, prison daughters served as a convenient substitute for birth children who, whether close or estranged, are physically not there.

Biological children

Generative participants who have children also expressed hope that their children's lives are good and will have some meaning. Yet, these women are not free to monitor the lives of their children as desired. The mother/child relationship during incarceration is a strained one. Maintaining contact, particularly with adult children, is often difficult and stressful; therefore, women in prison find it very frustrating and a little convoluted to try to encourage meaning and value while they are behind bars. Many of the older women were proud of their children. Some spoke about children who had graduated high school, had gone to college, had good jobs, and/or were handling their responsibilities very well. For others, their children were struggling with hardships and adjusting to the separation. Frances, a short-termer, lamented not being with her adult sons. She said, "Only thing I can do is share my wisdom." Many of the older women I spoke with reported they found it difficult to guide their children due to the difficulties associated with incarceration.

Nevertheless, the women often stressed education, finding good jobs, and staying out of trouble. Evelyn, a long-termer, was able to inspire her children to better themselves.

'They [my children] came to my graduation. I was speaker. My son wanted my tassel. I said "No, I worked hard to get it. You work hard too and when I get out – we'll hang them up together." He was going to quit school, but after that, he finished. My daughter had quit, but went back. My son is an engineer and daughter is a nurse.'

The women I interviewed reported sharing their experiences and what they learned, both for the betterment of their children and as evidence that they were making positive changes. One short-termer said, "When my kids visit, I preach to them about what I've learned in here." The last thing any of my participants wanted was for their children to follow their path to prison.

Talking to younger women was the most common generative act reported by the women in my sample. The forced interaction imposed by incarceration, while perhaps unpleasant due to noise and lack of privacy, certainly offers the opportunity to listen and share with others. Younger women provided the older ones with access to the future generation. Thus, many of the women I interviewed discussed their focus and genuine interest in improving the lives and outlooks of the younger participants. Generative behaviours regarding the betterment of society through future generations are therefore fairly easily accomplished in the prison environment. Yet, access to the larger society poses greater difficulty.

Sharing with others

As previously mentioned, some of the opportunities afforded to generative adults in free society are simply non-existent within the confines of the prison. Therefore, people who are incarcerated must be creative in finding generative outlets with which to help future generations and fulfil their desires to give back. Some of their expressions of generativity may be easily disregarded; they may be viewed as trivial by comparison to generativity outside of prison. Recall the definition of generativity as a commitment to the larger society and its continuation and/or improvement through the next generation. Sharing food with other residents may seem to be charity and *not* generativity, in view of that definition. I do not regard such behaviour as trivial, however. For the women I spoke with, sharing was a means of supporting others – which, at least for a time, functioned as their community. Betty said, "I've always helped people. Just because I'm here doesn't mean I can't. I try to turn negative to positive. Helps you make a change to help others make a change. Just help. Help each other. Get punished for it, but will still do it. It's called survival." I consider this behaviour to be *secondary generativity* because the participants spoke of these charitable actions as important to their sense of themselves and, what is more, their daily life behind bars. People in prison do not have easy access to free society, so 'giving back' to the prison community – other people in prison – provides them with an opportunity to do good and to feel good about themselves.

The older women I spoke with reported feeling good about themselves and their material ability to share with others. Betty, a long-termer, said, "Sharing is not allowed. If you need a drink, food, whatever, I'm giving it to you. Write me up. I'm doing it." Even small acts of kindness made the women feel needed and were often reported in conjunction with generative behaviours and desires.

Giving back to society

While generative people who are incarcerated may have limited access to the larger society, they contribute in ways available to them, such as programmes offered within the prison. Furthermore, the majority of the older women I spoke with had plans, upon their release, to share their experiences with youth in order to prevent them from going to prison. Thus, for my research participants, generativity was relevant at present and in the future. Some of the women had 20 years or more before their next parole hearing. Evelyn had just received a 20-year deferment. She declared, "I think I'll be a good influence when I get out, even if I'm 100 years old. I've set a goal. I'll do it." The older women in my sample shared a determination to give back to society.

Within prison

I can speak with no authority on the opportunities to contribute to the community offered at Pewee Valley. Specifics to the facility were not my focus and so I did not collect data on such. I can only mention the programmes as reported with little detail by my participants. Mable, a short-termer, stated, "I think about what I can give back. I think about talking to people. In here I make books in Braille which is another way to give back." Frances reported that she was on the inmate grievance committee, which gave her a sense of purpose. Clara, a long-termer worked in legal aid within the prison. She was proud of her ability to help others and offer them some hope for the future. Misty, a long-termer, seemed to take pride in her work of cleaning up for the members of the dog programme who train dogs for the disabled. The women I spoke with who participated in these programmes delighted in being able to make a difference.

After prison

The women in my sample commonly reported that they desired and planned to give something back to society upon their release. Most of the participants wanted to talk with youth and warn them about drugs and prison. Betty, a long-termer, remarked, "If you can help one kid, you've made one hell of an accomplishment. Kept one kid from going to prison. I want to do that. Something very positive. A way to give back." Rose said:

> 'I feel like it is something God wanted me to do. He put me in here to open my eyes – to go around and talk to younger kids. "I could save somebody's child." I'm going to get into helping young kids. Good kids out here trying. I might save them. There are too many addicts on

the street. People are always out there to tempt child with something. It may take somebody like me to stop it.'

Twenty-one of the women in my sample mentioned their plans for a generative future in response to my inquiry about how they saw themselves upon their release. Many of the women became very animated when talking to me about their plans to share with others. Anna declared, "I'm going to find some way to help other people. I want to do counselling and tell my story to kids. I want to tell my story and help other people. I want to help somebody else. I didn't have anybody to help me."

Some of the women shared plans of helping the prison community post-release. They desired to advocate for change and make things better for people in prison. Sue, a long-termer, declared, "I plan on volunteering in several organizations. I want to advocate for change in prison system. Tell my story to other people. I want to volunteer at church, AA, get a job. However, I need to give back, I'm going to do it. I want to be inspirational in helping other inmates." Anna, a short-termer, mentioned her desire to help people still in prison upon her release multiple times. She said, "I promise I will make a difference, if it is just to go to church and get hats and gloves for these women." For many of the women in my sample, planning their generative activities after their release gave them something to look forward to during their incarceration.

Legacy of an incarcerated woman

The women in my sample were confronting their own mortality and for some, it triggered thoughts concerning how they will be remembered. While I prompted my participants to discuss their legacy and how they will be remembered, over half of them admitted having thought about it several times before. For many, their legacy, as it stood, was not a good one, but that was something they were working on as best they could. Misty, a long-termer, observed:

> 'If I die today – if I didn't change, I would just leave them with me being a drug addict. I wanted to leave them something positive. I can't leave them material things, but I can leave them a better me. Not leaving a financial legacy but instead of leaving a legacy of what I came to prison for, I'm changing.'

Dalia discussed her contributions over the years:

Gina: Do you think about how you will be remembered?
Dalia: I think about it. I think I will be remembered for all the good things I've done in my life. I believe in helping others.

> I have good neighbors who help me. I'll be remembered as helping people. I go out of my way to help others. Neighbor's grandkids gave me a Christmas card. It said, 'for all the times you said, "Hi. Button up your coat", and played with us.' That meant a lot to me.

It was generally important for all of the women I spoke with to leave behind something better than what brought them to prison. They wanted to be remembered for their successes, not their failures.

This is why I'm here

Generative adults desire to promote the continuation and improvement of the larger society through the next generation: that is, they want to make a worthwhile difference. They are charged with the task of passing on the best of themselves – all the virtues they have acquired in their lives so far, such as their hope, their will, their purpose, their competence, and their love, to future generations.

The women I spoke with reported engaging in generative behaviours during incarceration. Unable to guide their own children, older women in prison often 'adopt' younger women. They pass on values, experience, and wisdom to the younger ones in hopes of improving their futures and preventing them from coming back to prison. They offer cautionary tales – encouraging them to 'do as I say, not as I did'. Furthermore, generative women plan to continue giving back upon their release. The women in my sample were almost consumed by thoughts of community service upon release – seemingly stemming from a desire to give back and make up for what they took. The women I spoke with were also concerned not only with how they would be remembered but also whether they would be remembered at all. Clearly, in order to be a generative person while incarcerated, one must confront and overcome obvious limitations and proactively seek out outlets such as community service programmes within the prison and utilize the access they have to future generations through younger women.

8

Why Not Give Them a Chance?

The purpose of this study was to explore the experiences of older women in prison, with a special focus on their experiences of generativity. The study findings support the salience of generative aspirations among older incarcerated women. The participants expressed their desire to give back to the community. They also reported concern for their own children and the children of others. The study also provides insight into how women are able to be generative behind bars. Finally, the findings also revealed several prison experiences that are unique to older women in prison.

Nearly all of the women in my sample were mothers and grandmothers. Their experiences of incarceration are unique compared to incarcerated women in general and certainly as compared to people in prison (men and women) even more generally, because they are very attached to their children *and* these children are grown. Most of what past research has found about the effects of incarceration on the mother/child relationship does not necessarily apply to older mothers with adult children. Rather than a straightforward dilemma of separation, the women in my sample varied in what the separation experience signified. They 'dealt' with motherhood behind bars in four ways. The *remorseful mother* regrets her past disregard for her children as a young mother and hopes to reconcile with her children. The *contented mother* enjoys a strong relationship with her children and reports being genuinely content with her current incarceration. The *uneasy mother* worries about the well-being of her adult children during the separation. Finally, the *abandoned mother* is surprised by her children's unexpected lack of support during her incarceration.

The women in my sample indicated that acceptance was a multifaceted concept. Three levels of acceptance were apparent: acceptance of incarceration, acceptance of responsibility, and acceptance of self. Many of the women I interviewed indicated that while they may not like being in prison, they had *accepted* it. Acceptance of incarceration eased the passing of time and often led to peace of mind. Acceptance of responsibility was mentioned by several participants; not that the emphasis on acceptance of responsibility may have been inculcated by prison-based rehabilitation programmes and self-help classes that emphasize this discourse. Finally, older participants described acceptance of self as an especially difficult kind of acceptance, one that allowed participants to feel good about themselves for the first time.

Generative desires extended beyond one's family in the free world, to fellow prison residents. The prison did not necessarily nurture such desires. Prisons, for the most part, are charged with keeping residents secure; therefore, they tend to encourage discipline and conformity more than they encourage gestures of generosity and goodwill. While Pewee Valley has several programmes which encourage generativity, such as dog training for the handicapped and making books in Braille for the blind, these programmes are not available for all residents. For example, those convicted of violent crimes are not eligible for the dog programme.

Jane, a long-termer, reported, "They told me on the Parole board that I should start thinking about myself, not others. ... I enjoy helping people. Tell me in here that I am too soft. Say I gotta quit that."

Older participants reported that prison staff members encourage them to take time to concentrate on themselves. Prisons offer self-discovery classes and treatment programmes to promote self-healing. Generativity is about putting others first, so generative people in prison often struggle with balancing self-recovery and their desires to selflessly help others.

Implications for policy

The study suggests that women in prison would gain much by having more service opportunities. The experiences of older women should figure into planning.

Use available resources, including educational, financial, and political, when developing generative programming. The negative social impacts of a growing prison population are becoming better known. Allowing people in prison to provide public service would be beneficial. Prison administrators have an opportunity to address barriers that might exist between society and people who are incarcerated, during and after incarceration. Stimulating and encouraging generative behaviours through programming can also ease one's reentry into society and potentially reduce recidivism. The blows that generative behaviours strike against a harmful carceral regime are no less valuable.

Structure generative programming so that people in prison begin their transition to post-prison life while still incarcerated. Prison administrators often view transition as a gradual process beginning at an individual's initial intake. Programming is structured to better enable prison residents to be successful upon release. Developing generative opportunities so individuals will interact with the same people who might work with them upon release offers powerful assistance with the transition back to society. For example, allowing incarcerated people to leave the prison in order to speak with students in public schools would also give them the needed contacts for a possible outlet to share and be generative upon release.

Accept both limitations and possibilities when considering how to provide generative opportunities. A variety of factors must be considered when determining how to provide generative opportunities, including the prison population, the corrections policies, and community and institutional potential. While not every individual who is incarcerated can or should be taken out of the facility and brought into free society, generative outlets may be implemented in other possible ways. Generative behaviours may be encouraged within the prison environment. Indeed, they are much needed there. For example, people in prison could be allowed to work on the sick ward in an effort to help their fellow prison residents. Mentoring programmes could also be implemented as a way of pairing older and younger people in prison together for the benefit of both but as a strong generative outlet for the older incarcerated people. Understanding what is possible within a particular institution requires tailoring programme offerings to a particular goal, such as generativity, and dropping the ideas that will not or cannot work.

Borrow lessons learned from other states and adapt them to fit programme goals. All states offering service opportunities will face similar questions regarding funding, community opportunities, cooperation and satisfaction, and effectiveness. While it is unreasonable to expect states to replicate programmes exactly (for example, the firefighting programme reported in Jehl [2000] is regionally specific), many of the ideals of these programmes can be utilized and modified for other states. Regardless of location, all states have community needs for which people in prison may be well-suited.

Document and learn from successes and failures. While various service programmes exist in numerous prisons across the country, these programmes have not been adequately evaluated for generative components and satisfaction and perception of people who are incarcerated. Though today some states more thoroughly document their efforts of rehabilitation through policy statements and research reports, too often the data are not collected. Understanding what works, and what does not work, in generative programming will help determine the development of future offerings.

Articulate the benefits of generativity so that outsiders understand. One purpose of this study was to explore generativity among people who are incarcerated, so naturally, the outside community has a vested interest in programming endeavours. Society should understand the potential benefits that generative programming can offer to the person who is incarcerated and to others. Reunification is often a difficult process, so programmes designed to ease that transition are beneficial to everyone. Articulating these benefits also ensures that policy makers would consider carefully before terminating such programmes.

Understand the needs surrounding motherhood among older women. Women with older children deal with separation differently than women with younger children: their experiences and needs should not be regarded as the same. For older women, the main issue is stable and functional support once they are released. Policy makers would benefit from identifying the different types of mother/child relationships and helping to strengthen weak or non-existent relationships, possibly as a means to reduce recidivism among older people.

Implications for further research

My research expands the knowledge base on older people in prison, incarcerated women, adaptation within prison, as well as generativity. My findings may interest life course criminologists who seek to understand intra-individual trajectories of offending and desistance. Life course criminologists Sampson and Laub (1992) write: 'Qualitative data derived from systematic open-ended questions or narrative life histories can help uncover underlying social processes of stability and change. They can also help to confirm the results derived from quantitative analyses' (p 80). Although my study does not relate generativity to subsequent offending (see Maruna, 2001), it does suggest connections between generativity and peaceable behaviour in prison, as generativity-minded older people who are incarcerated seek helping rather than harming opportunities behind bars.

Before turning to specifics of future research efforts I view as warranted, I would mention some clear *limitations* of my study. Parameters set by the prison authorities, last mentioned in Chapter 4, meant that I interviewed each participant once and for an average of two hours. The study may have benefited from follow-up interviews in order to obtain more detailed information about relevant but lesser topics of interest, such as criminal history and perceptions of prison health care. Furthermore, some participants seemed tired or somewhat disinterested in the interview. A follow-up interview may have caught them on a better day. I was only able to take hand-written notes during the interviews. Thus, the data may be incomplete due to my inability to document everything that the participants said. Audio recording would have allowed for more accurate transcription and, perhaps, more specific information.

My study concerns generativity, including the desire to give back. Generalizing from the study, it could be that older women in prison have a strong desire to give back. Alternatively, it is possible that those who volunteered to participate in the interview saw it as a generative opportunity, and thus, I have a bias in the form of a non-representative sample. This possibility was suggested by one participant, Sue, who told me, "I hope this study helps somebody. This is the first one [study] I've ever signed up for in 21½ years. I thought it could help." I cannot rule this possible source of bias out.

The study was a preliminary exploration of issues confronting older women in prison. It was not intended for generalization to the entire prison population or the rest of the women prison population. More standardized analyses are needed before any definitive conclusions can be made. The following are suggestions for additional research:

1. An equal number of younger and older participants should be included in order to determine if generativity is indeed age-specific within the prison population. All prison residents may exhibit some feelings or desires of restitution so the two concepts should be identified and separated to allow for a more accurate evaluation of feelings of generativity.
2. Gathering more information, and deploying different prompts to conversation, could help determine how race, sexuality, (past) poverty, and violent versus nonviolent history, shape – and impede or propel – generative desires and behaviours. My research participants did not frame their desires and behaviours in these terms, and I did not ask them to.
3. Researchers might conduct follow-up assessments of whether former prison residents *actually* seek to give back post-release. Having to delay generative efforts until after release might ultimately inhibit generative action. Or the generative desires of people in prison may be 'just talk'.
4. Surveys including reliable generativity scales should be implemented to accommodate larger samples and to provide statistical data for analysis. Very little research has been done that concerns generativity among older women in prison, qualitative *or* quantitative.
5. Identifying the types of motherhood among both older and younger women in prison may further understanding of social support of people who are incarcerated and identify ways to best assist women in different age groups during and after incarceration. For example, researchers may want to compare the types of motherhood indicated by this study with the experiences of younger incarcerated mothers. If the *uneasy mother* exists among younger mothers, it is not likely that she is uneasy in the same way or for the same reasons as the older mothers.

Final thoughts

For people in prison, participation in generative programmes is one link in a chain of positive events. The personal connections and support gained by participating in such service programmes may take them beyond the prison walls, providing the resources that people in prison need as they prepare to transition back into free society. Although this study began with my identifying generativity as not immediately associated with people in prison, the benefits of this type of programming reach beyond prison walls. That is, average citizens can play a part in giving people who are incarcerated a chance to give back what they have taken from their community.

Some who read this book may be dubious of the benefits of providing people in prison with more opportunities. The issue of fairness will always be considered in identifying services for incarcerated people, as the principle of 'least eligibility' demands that these not take resources such as job opportunities away from free citizens. However, many of the possible generative outlets would be voluntary. For many of my research participants, saving just one child from their incarcerated fate would be enough. I hope that this book provides a launching pad from which we might investigate ways of allowing people who are in prison wishing to 'give back' to achieve that goal. Subsequently, those who would provide such opportunities should measure, analyse and publish findings on the effectiveness of such programming and assess the perceptions of those on every side of the experience. Both quantitative and qualitative efforts are called for. Thus, I hope this study helps to stimulate the creation of more generative outlets for a small population of 'old-timers' who want to do good.

Afterword

Beth Easterling and Lois Presser

The manuscript that would eventually become this book was completed in December 2009. The author and our friend, Gina Benedict, first began framing her study of women in prison in 2007 – more than 15 years ago. Gina is no longer here with us to integrate new knowledge, from scholars and activists, related to carcerality and abolition, gender and intersections with other anchors of oppression (race, class, age, ability), harm and justice, parenthood, and stories – to name just a few relevant sites of inquiry. Nonetheless, we hope that readers appreciate Gina's incisive analysis and vital insights about women ageing in prison and giving back when one has little to give. In the pages that follow, we briefly comment on the study from the perspective of what Gina taught us and what issues remain quite open. The Appendix offers a compilation of newer publications in line with the topics of the book, as well as some older studies that may be of interest to readers.

On language

A common, ideological trope of criminology is to use the words 'offender', 'inmate', and 'prisoner' more or less interchangeably. Fundamentally, such terms erase the person. In addition, the fact of being in prison is conflated with the idea of having 'offended' – indeed, the idea of being an 'offender'. In her original dissertation/manuscript, Gina followed that convention. (Many of us are guilty of it.) We replaced nearly all such terms with person-first terminology, except when directly quoting a participant or describing previous research.

The terms female and women are likewise taken-for-granted nominalizations. In the space of time since Gina's writing, the two terms have become commonly understood as meaning different things. Relatively speaking, female is tied more to biology, and woman more to identity. Yet, female, used as a noun, is sometimes reductive, even a slur. Recalling our conversations with Gina, we determined that the women who were incarcerated at Pewee Valley and participated in this study self-identified as women. We footnote this information where Gina introduces her participants at the end of Chapter 1.

Throughout her work, we have updated wording to reflect the term 'woman' versus 'female' in most cases. However, in some cases when previous authors used the term female, we left Gina's descriptions as they were written.

Language carries the assumptions of the culture. Nothing can be represented neutrally, free of perspective; and perspectives that individuals seem to 'have' are always shaped collectively. We recalled that Gina tended to use the language of her participants, a fact that is now, too, footnoted where her research method is discussed. That decision is not neutral, but we put it out into the open. Keeping the participants' language true to their words, we think, was very important to Gina. As such, direct quotes and descriptions given by the participants in the study reflect their word choices.

Research focus

Gina designed minimally structured interviews. She 'took an exploratory approach and invited the women to discuss issues that were important to them' (p 9). Whereas Gina embarked on the study wondering how people in prison manage to make or find positive experiences there, she bracketed her interests in favour of a more inductive approach. But then, the majority of the older participants in Gina's study launched the topic of generativity themselves, though not in those terms. They spoke of ways they could give back despite being incarcerated; they expressed the idea that mothering and mentoring could help them achieve those goals. The study found its focus.

No researcher can cover all possible bases within any given project. Some readers may wonder how the study and its findings relate to knowledge in obviously pertinent fields including intersectionality, gerontology, and critical criminology. These approaches can and should be considered in connection with Gina Benedict's research.

Older women in prison exist and suffer at the intersection of several anchors of oppression including criminalization and carceral circumstance, gender, age, race, and often disability. Scholars who foreground intersectionality might consider the generative doings and plans of Gina's participants as ways in which subordinated bodies are recognizable as 'complex spaces of multiple meanings' (Nash, 2008, p 8).

Whereas Gina's 'older' participants are mostly middle aged, 'old age' is highly salient for them, a function of hard prison life and the prospect of years to come in prison. Gina's work pertains to gerontology and particularly critical studies of how 'old' gets constructed and what it means in multiple social spaces. Significantly, both 'old people' and imprisoned people are harmed by what Morganroth Gullette (2017) calls a 'duty-to-die ideology' (p 161).

Critical criminology is not explicitly mentioned in the book. However, readers will readily take note of the human rights implications of the work. Gina considered the use of existing programming and resources to support generative projects, such as community service, which would serve as a bridge to reentry. In the long term, or alternatively, these ideas may be taken as a bridge to abolition. Gina's study in no way redeems the carceral regime; it shows, rather, that people create meaning and joy regardless of its constraints.

Traditional prison researchers within criminology have paid considerable attention to coping, prisonization, and adaptation. Generativity may be considered a strong and creative mode of adaptation, the farthest reaches of coping. It constructs a story of being locked up at present into a better future. The concept of generativity comes from developmental psychology, with an emphasis on agency. The concept of adaptation to prison comes from sociology, with an emphasis on structure. Each realm of study – generativity and adaptation – can use more of what the other has to offer.

The co-construction of stories

Gina collaborated in the making of stories. On meeting each new interviewee, she shared that she was the mother of two young daughters. She explained, 'Motherhood provided a basis for relating: I intended it to encourage dialogue and it did' (p 8). Gina's methodological strategy invited sharing by the interviewees. It certainly would also have shaped what the stories would be about and how they would be told. She foregrounded parenting and concern for future generations. Yet, Gina could not have avoided shaping the data, for human beings construct themselves in and through encounters, and use whatever is at hand to do so. Gina's interviewees would, inevitably, take her greeting to construct the self they aspired to be.

In this regard, Presser (2008) notes that qualitative researchers become 'co-producers' of their data. Narratives in particular are understood as tailored to the circumstances of telling. As Gubrium and Holstein (2009) put it, they are formed 'at the confluence of respect and sociability' (p 201). Gina's opening gambit about being a mother set a tone of sociability premised on a social role in common – that of nurturing others. As for respect, Gina set a high bar, always. Hollway and Jefferson (2000) offer relevant insight concerning the influence of respect on research interviews: 'Questions concerning trust and respect are constantly at issue and at any moment can change the direction of what is said and the meanings that are exchanged' (p 88). A giving, meaningful life was thematized across Gina's interviews with older women. That theme cannot easily be detached from Gina's own giving, meaningful life.

Final thoughts

Gina never neglected to thank others for the support they gave her. So we want to end this book in that spirit and in Gina's own words. I conclude with her dissertation acknowledgements.

I would like to thank Dr Lois Presser for her assistance throughout this project. As a person, Dr Presser is remarkable and as a mentor, she is exceptional. Her guidance, encouragement, and support were invaluable in helping me to complete this project. I would also like to thank Dr Allison Anders, Dr Damayanti Banerjee, Dr Michael Braswell, and Dr Ben Feldmeyer for serving as members of my dissertation committee and for offering helpful suggestions in order to improve this project. In addition, thank you to the faculty of the Department of Sociology for making the last four years a rewarding and valuable learning experience, with special thanks to Betty Lou and Millie for their assistance, friendship, and welcoming smiles throughout my tenure as a graduate student. I would also like to thank my dear friends Stacey and Sarah for providing me with empathy and good times – I will always be available for lunch. I would like to thank 'Aunt' Pat for her continued support and love as I pursued my goal. Thank you to my parents, Mickey and Cookie, for their unwavering support, infinite love, and constant encouragement in all of my endeavors. They are an inspiration to me and have given me the confidence and drive to pursue and obtain an advanced degree. Thank you to Michael for being my big brother – someone who has always given me encouragement, strength, and laughter when I needed them most. I would like to thank my husband, Travis, whose patience, understanding, and love mean the world to me. A special thank you to my daughters, Zoe and Mia, who showed an incredible amount of understanding for being so young – Mommy loves you.

– Regina 'Gina' White Benedict, 2009

References

Gubrium, J. F. & J. A. Holstein. 2009. *Analyzing Narrative Reality*. Los Angeles: SAGE.

Hollway, W. & T. Jefferson. 2000. *Doing Qualitative Research Differently: Free Association, Narrative and the Interview Method*. London: SAGE.

Morganroth Gullette, M. 2017. *Ending Ageism, or How Not to Shoot Old People*. New Brunswick, NJ: Rutgers University Press.

Nash, J. C. 2008. 'Re-Thinking Intersectionality'. *Feminist Review*, 89(1): 1–15.

Presser, L. 2008. *Been a Heavy Life: Stories of Violent Men*. Urbana, IL and Chicago, IL: University of Illinois Press.

APPENDIX A

Sample Demographics and Details of Current Sentence

Pseudonym	Age	Race	Number of children	Sentence (years)	Conviction charge(s)
Anna	53	Black	5	1	Possession, Probation Violation
Betty	43	White	3	Life	Child Neglect, Intent to Murder
Carol	42	Black	4	8	Assault, Robbery Second Degree
Christy	34	White	2	10	Sex Offender, Probation Violation
Clara	65	White	5	530	Sodomy 1, Sodomy 2, First-Degree Incest (Multiple Counts)
Dalia	45	Black	2	17½	Trafficking Controlled Substance, Parole Violation
Doris	62	White	1	1	Forged Prescription
Elle	51	Black	0	20	First-Degree Manslaughter, Parole Violation
Eve	41	White	2	Life	Complicity to Commit Murder, First-Degree Robbery
Evelyn	44	White	2	70	Murder and Attempted Murder
Frances	53	White	2	12	First-Degree Assault, Criminal Facilitation
Jane	55	White	3	15	Second-Degree Manslaughter
Jo	39	White	1	20	Criminal Attempted Murder

APPENDIX A

Pseudonym	Age	Race	Number of children	Sentence (years)	Conviction charge(s)
Joy	52	Black	2	7	Felony Possession, Probation Violation
June	52	White	2	2	Theft by Deception, Probation Violation
Katherine	50	White	1	10	Arson/Insurance Fraud
Kay	52	White	2	14	Drug Charge, Possession of Firearm
Mable	53	White	2	8	Trafficking Prescription Drugs
Margaret	50	White	2	4	Alluding Police
Mary	54	Black	2	5	Possession of Controlled Substance
May	50	Black	3	12	Trafficking Controlled Substance
Misty	50	White	4	Life	First-Degree Murder
Peggy	58	White	0	12	Trafficking of Controlled Substance, Probation Violation
Polly	44	White	2	15	Assault
Rose	60	Black	2	13	Manslaughter
Sally	53	White	2	7	Trafficking of Controlled Substance and Possession
Sarah	27	Black	2	10	First Degree Robbery
Stella	52	White	3	3	Robbery
Sue	54	White	3	Life	Kidnapping, Criminal Conspiracy, Robbery, Facilitation to Rape and Murder

APPENDIX B

Research Synopsis

Hello:

I invite you to participate in a study on your life experiences in and out of prison. If you choose to participate, you will be scheduled for an interview lasting up to two hours. The interviews will be conducted in a secure location which is separate from the general population. Your privacy and the confidentiality of your answers and comments will be honoured. When I report results, I may describe specific discussions or include direct quotes, but I will not use your real name or any other identifying information. Please let prison staff know of your interest to participate.

Sincerely,
Regina Benedict
Doctoral candidate
University of Tennessee-Knoxville

APPENDIX C

Suggestions for Further Reading

Avieli, H. 2021. '"A Sense of Purpose": Older Prisoners' Experiences of Successful Aging Behind Bars'. *European Journal of Criminology,* 19(6): 1660–1677. https://doi.org/10.1177/1477370821995142.

Baldwin, L. 2018. 'Motherhood Disrupted'. *Emotion, Space, and Society,* 26: 49–56.

Canada, K. E., Barrenger, S. L., Robinson, E. L., Washington, K. T., & Mills, T. 2020. 'A Systematic Review of Interventions for Older Adults Living in Jails and Prisons'. *Aging & Mental Health,* 24(7): 1019–1029. https://doi.org/10.1080/13607863.2019.1584879.

Danely, J. 2022. 'What Older Prisoners Teach Us About Care and Justice in an Aging World'. *Anthropology and Aging,* 43(1): 58–65.

Hoskins, K. M. 2018. 'Women Offenders' Response to Victimization and Trauma and its Relationship with Satisfaction in Life, Mental Illness, and Substance use'. Unpublished Dissertation: ProQuest. Retrieved from: https://www.proquest.com/openview/a0dd18d3f0e1fd15e6acaf18e368e8c8/1?pq-origsite=gscholar&cbl=18750

Humblet, D. 2021. '"Thriving" in Prison in Old Age'. In D. Humblet, *The Older Prisoner.* Cham: Palgrave MacMillan.

Lemieux, C. M., Dyeson, T. B., & Castiglione, B. 2002. 'Revisiting the Literature of Prisoners Who Are Older: Are We Wiser?' *The Prison Journal,* 82(4): 440–458.

Maschi, T. & Morgen, K. 2020. *Aging behind Prison Walls: Studies in Trauma and Resilience.* New York: Columbia University Press.

Masson, I., Baldwin, L., & Booth, N. (eds). 2021. *Critical Reflections on Women, Family, Crime and Justice.* Bristol: Bristol University Press.

Nagy, V. 2020. 'Women, Old Age, and Imprisonment in Victoria, Australia 1860–1920'. *Women & Criminal Justice,* 30(3): 155–171.

Nixon, S. 2019. '"I Just Want to Give Something Back": Peer Work in Prison'. *Prison Service Journal,* 245: 44–53.

Smoyer, A. B., Madera, J. E., & Blankenship, K. M. 2019. 'Older Adults Lived Experience of Incarceration'. *Journal of Offender Rehabilitation*, 58(3): 220–229. https://doi.org/10.1080/10509674.2019.1582574.

Wahidin, A. 2002. 'Reconfiguring Older Bodies in the Prison Time Machine'. *Journal of Aging and Identity*, 7: 177–193.

References

Aday, R. 1994. 'Golden Years Behind Bars: Programs and Facilities for the Geriatric Inmate'. *Federal Probation*, 58(2): 47–54.

Aday, R. 1995. *A Preliminary Report on Mississippi's Elderly Prison Population*. Parchment, MS: Mississippi Department of Corrections.

Aday, R. 1999. 'Responding to the Graying of American Prisons: A 10-year Follow-up'. Unpublished report. Murfreesboro, TN: Middle Tennessee State University.

Aday, R. 2001. 'A Comprehensive Health Assessment of Aged and Infirm Inmates'. Nashville, TN: Tennessee Department of Correction.

Aday, R. 2003. *Aging Prisoners: Crisis in American Corrections*. London: Praeger.

Aday, R. 2006. 'Aging Prisoners' Concerns toward Dying in Prison'. *OMEGA*, 52(3): 199–216.

Aday, R. & M. Huey Dye. 2018. 'Examining Predictors of Depression among Older Incarcerated Women'. *Women & Criminal Justice*. Available from: https://doi.org./10.1080/08974454.2018.1443870

Aday, R. & P. Nation. 2001. *A Case Study of Older Female Offenders*. Nashville, TN: Tennessee Department of Correction.

Aday, R. & J. Krabill. 2011. *Women Aging in Prison: A Neglected Population in the Correctional System*. Boulder, CO: Lynne Rienner.

Aday, R., J. Krabill, & D. Deaton-Owens. 2014. 'Religion in the Lives of Older Women Serving Life in Prison'. *Journal of Women & Aging*, 26(3): 238–256.

Aldous, J. 1995. 'New Views of Grandparents in an Intergenerational Context'. *Journal of Family Issues*, 16: 104–122.

AMA White Paper on Elderly Health. 1990. *Arch Internal Medicine*, 150: 2459–2472. Chicago, IL: American Medical Association.

American Correctional Association. 2012. *Directory of Adult Correctional Facilities*. Lanham, MD: American Correctional Association.

Amnesty International. 1999. 'United States of America: Not Part of My Sentence – Violations of the Human Rights of Women in Custody American Correctional Association. 2012 *Directory of Adult Correctional Facilities*. Lanham, MD. Available from: www.web.amnesty.org

Anderson, T. 2003. 'Issues in the Availability of Health Care for Women Prisoners'. In S. Sharp, ed., *The Incarcerated Woman*, pp. 49–60. Upper Saddle River, NJ: Prentice Hall.

Arnold, D., W. Dobbie, & P. Hull. 2022. 'Measuring Racial Discrimination in Bail Decisions'. *American Economic Review*, 112 (9): 2992–3038.

Bachand, D. 1984. 'The Elderly Offender: An Exploratory Study with Implications for Continuing Education of Law Enforcement Personnel'. Unpublished doctoral dissertation, Ann Arbor, MI: University of Michigan.

Badgio, P. & B. Worden. 2007. 'Cognitive Functioning and Aging in Women'. *Journal of Women & Aging*, 19(1/2): 13–30.

Baltes, P. & K. Mayer. 1999. *The Berlin Aging Study: Aging from 70 to 100*. Cambridge: Cambridge University Press.

Barnett, R. & G.K. Baruch. 1978. 'Women in the Middle Years: A Critique of Research and Theory'. *Psychology of Women Quarterly*, 3: 187–197.

Baro, A. 1997. 'Spheres of Consent: An Analysis of the Sexual Abuse and Sexual Exploitation of Women Incarcerated in the State of Hawaii'. *Women & Criminal Justice*, 8: 61–84.

Baunach, P. 1985. *Mothers in Prison*. New Brunswick, NJ: Transaction.

Baunach, P. 1992. 'Critical Problems of Women in Prison'. In I. Moyer, ed., *The Changing Roles of Women in the Criminal Justice System*, pp. 99–112. Prospect Heights, IL: Waveland Press.

Belknap, J. 2007. *The Invisible Woman: Gender, Crime, and Justice*, 3rd Ed. Belmont, CA: Wadsworth.

Black, H. K., & R. L. Rubinstein. 2009. 'The Effect of Suffering on Generativity: Accounts of Elderly African American Men'. *The Journals of Gerontology: Series B*, 64B (2): 296–303.

Bloom, B. & D. Steinhart. 1993. *Why Punish the Children? A Reappraisal of the Children of Incarcerated Mothers in America*. San Francisco: National Council on Crime and Delinquency.

Bond, G. D., L. A. Thompson, & D. M. Malloy. 2005. 'Lifespan Differences in the Social Networks of Prison Inmates'. *International Journal of Aging and Human Development*, 61(3): 161–178.

Booth, D. 1989. 'Health Status of the Incarcerated Elderly: Issues and Concerns'. *Journal of Offender Counseling, Services and Rehabilitation*, 13: 193–214.

Bosworth, M. 2003. 'Gender, Race, and Sexuality in Prison'. In B. Zaitzow and J. Thomas, eds., *Women in Prison: Gender and Social Control*, pp. 137–154. Boulder, CO: Lynne Rienner.

Bronfenbrenner, U., P. McClelland, E. Wethington, P. Moen & S. J. Ceci. 1996. *The State of Americans: The Disturbing Facts and Figures on Changing Values, Crime, The Economy, Poverty, Family, Education, The Aging Population, and What they Mean for Our Future*. New York, NY: The Free Press.

Brown, J. 1991. 'The Professional Ex: An Alternative for Exiting the Deviant Career'. *The Sociological Quarterly*, 32: 219–230.

Browne, A., B. Miller, & E. Maguire. 1999. 'Prevalence and Severity of Lifetime Physical and Sexual Abuse among Incarcerated Women'. *International Journal of Law and Psychiatry* 22(3–4): 301–322.

Browning, D. 1975. *Generative Man: Psychoanalytic Perspectives*. New York: Dell.

Bureau of Justice Statistics. 2000. *Incarcerated Parents and Their Children*. Washington, DC: U.S. Department of Justice.

Bureau of Justice Statistics. 2001. *Prisoners at Midyear 2000*. Washington, DC: U.S. Department of Justice.

Caddick, B. 1994. 'The 'New Careers' Experiment in Rehabilitating Offenders: Last Messages From a Fading Star'. *British Journal of Social Work*, 24: 449–460.

Caldwell, C., M. Jarvis, & H. Rosefield. 2001. 'Issues Impacting Today's Geriatric Female Offenders'. *Corrections Today*, 65(5): 110–113.

Carmel, S. (2019). 'Health and Well-Being in Later Life: Gender Differences Worldwide'. *Frontiers in Medicine*, 6. Available from: https://doi.org/10.3389/fmed.2019.00218

Carson, E. A. 2020. *Prisoners in 2019*. (NCJ 255115). US Department of Justice: Bureau of Justice Statistics.

Carstensen, L. L. 1992. 'Social and Emotional Patterns in Adulthood: Support for Socioemotional Selectivity Theory'. *Psychology & Aging,* 7(3): 331–338.

Carter, B. 1981. 'Reform School Families'. In L. Bowker, ed., *Women and Crime*, pp. 419–431. New York: Macmillan.

Cavanaugh, J. & F. Blanchard-Fields. 2002. *Adult Development and Aging*. Belmont, CA: Wadsworth/Thompson Learning.

Chesney-Lind, M. 1997. *The Female Offender: Girls, Women, and Crime*. Thousand Oaks, CA: Sage.

Church, G. 1990. 'The View from behind Bars'. *Time Magazine* (Fall) 135: 20–22.

Clark, J. 1995. 'The Impact of the Prison Environment on Mothers'. *Prison Journal*, 75(3) (September): 306–329.

Clemmer, D. 1940. *The Prison Community*. New York: Holt, Rinehart, & Winston.

Colsher, P., R. Wallace, P. Loeffelholz, & M. Sales. 1992. 'Health Status of Older Male Prisoners: A Comprehensive Survey'. *American Journal of Public Health*, 82: 881–884.

Crawley, E. 2005. 'Institutional Thoughtlessness in Prisons and Its Impacts on the Day-to-Day Lives of Elderly Men'. *Journal of Contemporary Criminal Justice*, 21(4): 350–363.

Crosnoe, R. & G. Elder. 2002. 'Successful Adaptation in the Later Years: A Life Course Approach to Aging'. *Social Psychology Quarterly*, 65(4): 309–328.

Davoren, M., M. Fitzpatrick, F. Caddow, M. Caddow, C. O'Neill, & H. G. Kennedy. 2015. 'Older Men and Older Women Remand Prisoners: Mental Illness, Physical Illness, Offending Patterns and Needs'. *International Psychogeriatrics*, 27(5): 747–755.

de St. Aubin, E., D. McAdams, & T. Kim. 2004. 'The Generative Society: An Introduction'. In E. de St. Aubin, D. McAdams, & T. Kim, eds., *The Generative Society: Caring for Future Generations*, pp. 3–14. Washington DC: American Psychological Association.

Dellmann-Jenkins, M., M. Blankemeyer, & O. Pinkard. 2000. 'Young Adult Children and Grandchildren in Primary Caregiver Roles to Older Relatives and Their Service Needs'. *Family Relations: Interdisciplinary Journal of Applied Family Science*, 49(2): 177–186.

Dickey, W. & M. Smith. 1998. *Dangerous Opportunity: Five Futures for Community Corrections: The Report From the Focus Group*. Washington, DC: U.S. Department of Justice, Office of Justice Programs.

Ditton, P. 1999. *Mental Health and Treatment of Inmates and Probationers*. Washington, DC: Bureau of Justice Statistics.

Dholakia, N. 2021. 'Women's Incarceration Rates are Skyrocketing. These Advocates Are Trying to Change That'. Vera Institute of Justice, May 17. Available from: www.vera.org/news/womens-voices/womens-incarceration-rates-are-skyrocketing

Douglass, R. 1991. *Oldtimers: Michigan's Elderly Prisoners*. Lansing, MI: Michigan Department of Corrections.

Dressel, P. L. & S. Barnhill. 1994. 'Reframing Gerontological Thought and Practice: The Case of Grandmothers with Daughters in Prisons'. *The Gerontologist*, 34(5): 685–691. Available from: https://doi-org.myezproxy.vub.ac.be/10.1093/geront/34.5.685

Easterling, B. A., L. Presser, & B. Feldmeyer. 2021. 'Storying Motherhood from Prison'. In L. Carter, C. Blankenship, & C. Marcum eds., *Punishing Gender Past and Present: Examining the Criminal Justice System across Gendered Experiences*. San Diego, CA: Cognella Academic Publishing.

Ebersole, P. & P. Hess. 1998. *Toward Healthy Aging*. St. Louis, IL: Mosby.

Ekstrand, C., D. Burton, & E. Erdman. 1999. *Women in Prison: Issues and Challenges Confronting U.S. Correctional Systems*. Washington, DC: General Accounting Office.

Enos, S. 2001. *Mothering from the Inside: Parenting in a Women's Prison*. Albany, NY: State University of New York Press.

Erikson, E. 1950. *Childhood and Society*. New York: Norton.

Erikson, E. 1963. *Childhood and Society*, 2nd Ed. New York: Norton.

Erikson, E. 1969. *Gandhi's Truth: On the Origins of Militant Nonviolence*. New York: Norton.

Erikson, E., J. M. Erikson, & H. Q. Kivnick. 1986. *Vital Involvement in Old Age*. New York: Norton.

Fader, J. J., A. Henson, & J. Brey. 2022. '"I Don't Want to Be a Statistic": Racial-Criminal Stigma, Redemption Bids, and Redemptive Generativity'. *Crime & Delinquency*, 1–26. Online first: https://doi.org/10.1177/00111287221131

REFERENCES

Falter, R. 1999. 'Selected Predictors of Health Service Needs of Inmates over Age 50'. *Journal of Correctional Health Care*, 6: 149–175.

Farley, M. & V. Kelly. 2000. 'Prostitution: A Critical Review of the Medical and Social Sciences Literature'. *Women & Criminal Justice*, 11: 29–64.

Farrell, A. 1998. 'Mothers, Offending Against Their Role: An Australian Experience'. *Women & Criminal Justice*, 9: 47–69.

Ferraro, K. & A. Moe. 2003. 'Malign Neglect of Benign Respect: Women's Health Care in a Carceral Setting'. *Women & Criminal Justice* 14(4): 9–40.

Fletcher, B. & D. Moon. 1993. 'Introduction'. In B. Fetcher, L. Shaver, & D. Moon, eds., *Women Prisoners: A Forgotten Population*, pp. 5–14. Westport, CT: Praeger.

Fox, J. 1975. 'Women in Crisis'. In H. Toch, ed., *Man in Crisis*, pp. 181–205. Chicago, IL: Aldine-Atherton.

Fox, J. 1984. 'Women's Prison Policy, Prisoner Activism, and the Impact of the Contemporary Feminist Movement: A Case Study'. *Prison Journal*, 64(1): 15–36.

Frankl, V. E. 1984. *Man's Search for Meaning: An Introduction to Logotherapy*, 3rd Ed. New York: Simon & Schuster.

Gannon, L. 1999. *Women and Aging*. New York: Routledge.

Genders, E. & E. Player. 1990. 'Women Lifers: Assessing the Experience'. *Prison Journal*, 80(1): 46–57.

Giallombardo, R. 1966. 'Interviewing in the Prison Community'. *Journal of Criminal Law, Criminology, and Police Science*, 57(3): 318–324.

Gilleard, C. & P. Higgs. 2016. 'Connecting Life Span Development with the Sociology of the Life Course: A New Direction'. *Sociology*, 50(2): 301–315. doi: 10.1177/0038038515577906.

Gilligan, C. 1982. *In a Different Voice: Psychological Theory and Women's Development*. Cambridge, MA: Harvard University Press.

Girshick, L. 1999. *No Safe Haven: Stories of Women in Prison*. Boston, MA: Northeastern University Press.

Haesen, S., H. Merkt, A.Imber, B. Elger, & T. Wangmo (2019). 'Substance Use and Other Mental Health Disorders among Older Prisoners'. *International Journal of Law and Psychiatry*, 62: 20–31.

Halsey, M. & V. Harris. 2011. 'Prisoner Futures: Sensing the Signs of Generativity'. *Australian & New Zealand Journal of Criminology*, 44(1) 74–93.

Hamm, M. 1997. 'The Offender Self-Help Movement as Correctional Treatment'. In P. Van Voorhis, M. Braswell, & D. Lester, eds., *Correctional Counseling and Rehabilitation*, 4th Ed. pp. 211–224. Cincinnati, OH: Anderson.

Handtke, V., W. Bretchneider, B. Elger, & T. Wangmo. 2015. Easily Forgotten: Elderly Female Prisoners'. *Journal of Aging Studies*, 32: 1–11.

Hanke, P. & C. Faupel. 'Women Opiate Users' Perceptions of Treatment Services in New York City'. *Journal of Substance Abuse Treatment*, 10(6): 513–522.

Harris, J. 1988. *They Always Call Us Ladies.* New York: Kensington.

Hart, C. 1995. 'Gender Differences in Social Support among Inmates'. *Women & Criminal Justice,* 6: 67–88.

Hart, H. M., D. P. McAdams, B. J. Hirsch, & J. J. Bauer. 2001. 'Generativity and Social Involvement among African Americans and White Adults'. *Journal of Research in Personality,* 35: 208–230.

Hatch, L. 2005. 'Gender and Ageism'. *Generations,* 29(3): 19–24.

Haug, M. & S. Folmar. 1986. 'Longevity, Gender, and Life Quality'. *Journal of Health and Social Behavior,* 27: 332–345.

Heffernan, E. 1972. *Making It in Prison: The Square, the Cool, and the Life.* New York: John Wiley and Sons.

Heimer, K., S. E. Malone, & S. De Coster. 2022. 'Trends in Women's Incarceration Rates in US Prisons and Jails: A Tale of Inequalities'. *Annual Review of Criminology,* 6. Online first: https://doi.org/10.1146/annurev-criminol-030421-041559

Henderson, D. J. 1998. 'Drug Abuse and Incarcerated Women: A Research Review'. *Journal of Substance Abuse Treatment,* 15(6): 579–587.

Henriques, Z. 1996. 'Imprisoned Mothers and Their Children: Separation-Reunion Syndrome Dual Impact'. *Women and Criminal Justice,* 8(1): 77–95.

Holley, P. & D. Brewster. 1996. 'The Women at Eddie Warrior Correctional Center: Descriptions from a Data Set'. *Journal of the Oklahoma Criminal Justice Research Consortium,* 3: 107–114.

Holt, K. 1982. 'Nine Months of Life: The Law and the Pregnant Inmate'. *Journal of Family Law,* 20(3): 523–543.

Holtzman, J., A. Brauger, & C. Jones. 1987. 'Health Care of Older Women and Minorities: Implications for Education and Training Programs'. In G. Lesnoff-Caravagua, ed., *Handbook of Applied Gerontology.* New York: Human Service Press.

Hooyman, N. & H. Kiyak. 2002. *Social Gerontology.* Boston, MA: Allyn & Bacon.

House, J., D. Umberson, & K. Landis. 'Structures and Processes of Social Support'. *Annual Review of Sociology,* 14: 293–318.

Human Rights Watch. 1996. 'All Too Familiar: Sexual Abuse or Women in U.S. State Prisons'. Available from: www.hru.org/hrw

Humblet, D. 2021. '"Thriving" in prison in old age'. In: *The Older Prisoner.* Palgrave Studies in Prison and Penology. London: Palgrave MacMillan. Available from: https://doi.org/10.1007/978-3-030-60120-1_6

Irwin, J. 1970. *The Felon.* Englewood Cliffs, NJ: Prentice Hall.

Irwin, J. 1980. *Prisons in Turmoil.* Boston, MA: Little, Brown.

Irwin, J. & D. R. Cressey. 1962. 'Thieves, Convicts, and the Inmate Culture'. *Social Problems,* 10, 142–155.

Jehl, D. 2000. 'Inmates Battling West's Fires Help States and Themselves'. *New York Times,* September 5, p. A1.

Johnston, D. 1995. 'Jailed Mothers'. In K. Gabel & D. Johnston, eds., *Children of Incarcerated Parents*, pp. 41–55. New York: Lexington.

Kashy, D. A. & M. Morash. 2022. 'Predictors of Generativity and Satisfaction with Life in a Sample of Women Offenders'. *Psychology, Crime, & Law*, 6: 587–607. Available from: doi.org/10.1080/1068316X.2021.1929981

Koban, L. 1983. 'Parents in Prison: A Comparative Analysis of the Effects of Incarceration on the Families of Men and Women'. *Research in Law, Deviance, and Social Control*, 5: 171–183.

Koenig, H., S. Johnson, J. Bellard, M. Denker, & R. Fenlon. 1995. 'Depression and Anxiety Disorder among Older Male Inmates at a Federal Correctional Facility'. *Psychiatric Services*, 46(4): 339–401.

Kolker, C. 2000. 'Prison Hospices on Increase; Aid Dying Inmates, Cut Violence'. *Schenectady Gazette*, February 6, pp. H1–H2.

Kotre, J. 1984. *Outliving the Self: Generativity and the Interpretation of Lives*. Baltimore, MD: Johns Hopkins University Press.

Kovera, M. B. 2019. 'Racial Disparities in the Criminal Justice System'. *Journal of Social Issues*, 75(4): 1139–1164.

Krabill, J. J. & R. H. Aday. 2005. 'Exploring the Social World of Aging Female Prisoners'. *Women & Criminal Justice*, 1: 27–53. Available from: https://doi.org/10.1300/J012v17n01_02

Kratcoski, P. & S. Babb. 1990. 'Adjustment of Older Inmates: An Analysis by Institutional Structure and Gender'. *Journal of Contemporary Criminal Justice*, 6: 139–156.

Kreager, D. A., J. T. N. Young, D. L. Haynie, M. Bouchard, D. R. Schaefer, & G. Zajac. 2017. 'Where "Old Heads" Prevail: Inmate Hierarchy in a Men's Prison Unit'. *American Sociological Review*, 82(4): 685–718.

Lanier, C. 2003. '"Who's Doing the Time Here, Me or My Children?": Addressing the Issues Implicated by Mounting Numbers of Fathers in Prison'. In J. Ross & S. Richards, eds., *Convict Criminology*, pp. 170–190. Belmont, CA: Wadsworth.

Larson, J. H. & J. Nelson. 1984. 'Women, Friendship, and Adaptation to Prison'. *Jounral of Criminal Justice*, 12(6), 601–615.

Leonard, E. 1983. 'Judicial Decisions and Prison Reform: The Impact of Litigation on Women's Prisons'. *Social Problems*, 31(October): 45–58.

Letherby. G. 2003. *Feminist Research in Theory and Practice*. Buckingham: Open University Press.

Lindquist, C. & C. Lindquist. 1999. 'Health Behind Bars: Utilization and Evaluation of Medical Care among Jail Inmates'. *Journal of Community Health*, 24(4): 285–303.

Maeve, K. 1999. 'Adjudicated Health: Incarcerated Women and the Social Construction of Health'. *Crime, Law, and Social Change*, 31: 49–71.

Mahan. S. 1984. 'Imposition of Despair: An Ethnography of Women in Prison'. *Justice Quarterly*, 1: 357–384.

Malloch, M. 2000. *Women, Drugs, and Custody: The Experiences of Women Drug Users in Prison*. Winchester: Waterside Press.

Mann, C.R. 1984. *Female Crime and Delinquency*. Tuscaloosa, AL: University of Alabama Press.

Marcus-Mendoza, S. & E. Wright. 2003. 'Treating the Woman'. In S. Sharp, ed., *The Incarcerated Woman*, pp. 107–117. Upper Saddle River, NJ: Prentice Hall.

Markides, K. 1992. 'Risk Factors, Gender, and Health'. In J. Hendricks and L. Glasse, eds., *Gender and Aging*, pp. 25–43. Amityville, NY: Baywood.

Maruna, S. 2001. *Making Good: How Ex-Convicts Reform and Rebuild Their Lives*. Washington, DC: American Psychological Association.

Maruna, S., T. LeBel, & C. Lanier. 2004. 'Generativity Behind Bars: Some "Redemptive Truth" About Prison Society'. In E. de St. Aubin, D. McAdams, T. Kim, eds., *The Generative Society: Caring for Future Generations*, pp. 131–151. Washington, DC: American Psychological Association.

Maschi, T. & K. Morgen. 2020. *Aging behind Prison Walls: Studies in Trauma and Resilience*. New York: Columbia University Press.

McAdams, D. 1985. *Power, Intimacy, and the Life Story: Personological Inquiries into Identity*. New York: Guilford.

McAdams, D. & E. de St. Aubin. 1992. 'A Theory of Generativity and Its Assessment through Self-report, Behavioral Acts, and Narrative Themes in Autobiography'. *Journal of Personality and Social Psychology*, 62: 1003–1015.

McAdams, D. & J. Azarow. 1996. 'Generativity in Black and White: Relations Among Generativity, Race, and Well-Being'. Paper presented at the Annual Meeting of the American Psychological Association, Toronto, Canada.

McAdams, D., H. Hart, & S. Maruna. 1998. 'The Anatomy of Generativity'. In D. McAdams and E. de St. Aubin, eds., *Generativity and Adult Development*, pp. 7–43. Washington DC: American Psychological Association.

McAdams, D. & R. Logan. 2004. 'What Is Generativity'? In E. de St. Aubin, D. McAdams, & T. Kim, eds., *The Generative Society: Caring for Future Generations*, pp. 15–32. Washington DC: American Psychological Association.

McCarthy, M. 1983. 'The Health Status of Elderly Inmates'. *Corrections Today*, 45: 64–65.

McClellan, D. 1994. 'Disparity in the Discipline of Male and Female Inmates in Texas Prisons'. *Women and Criminal Justice*, 5(2): 71–97.

McKillop, M. & A. Boucher. 2018. *Aging Prison Populations Drive Up Costs*. Philadelphia: The Pew Charitable Trusts.

Memoirs of the National Academy of Science, Vol. XV, *Psychological Testing in the United States Army*, Robert M. Yerkes, ed., Government Printing Office, Washington, DC, 1921, p. 790.

Millen, D. 1997. 'Some Methodological and Epistemological Issues Raised by Doing Feminist Research on Non-Feminist Women'. *Sociological Research Online*, 2(3). Available from: www.socresonline.org,uk/socresonline/2/3/3.html

Miller, D. 1990. 'Women in Pain: Substance Abuse/Self-Medication'. In M. Mirkin, ed., *The Social and Political Contexts of Family Therapy*, pp. 179–192. Boston, MA: Allyn & Bacon.

Moe, A. & K. Ferraro. 2003. 'Malign Neglect of Benign Respect: Women's Health Care in a Carceral Setting'. *Women & Criminal Justice*, 14: 53–80.

Moon, D., R. Thompson, & R. Bennett. 'Patterns of Substance Use among Women In Prison'. In B. Fetcher, L. Shaver, & D. Moon, eds., *Women Prisoners: A Forgotten Population*, pp. 45–54. Westport, CT: Praeger.

Morash, M. & P. J. Schram. 2002. *The Prison Experience: Special Issues of Women in Prison*. Prospect Heights, IL: Waveland Press

Morris, A. 1987. *Women, Crime, and Criminal Justice*. Oxford: Basil Blackwell.

Morton, J. 1992. 'An Administrative Overview of the Older Inmate'. Department of Justice, National Institute of Corrections.

Mumma, H. & E. Smith. 1981. *The Geriatric Assistant*. New York: McGraw-Hill.

Nellis, A. 2021. *The Color of Justice: Racial and Ethnic Disparity in State Prisons*. Washington, DC: The Sentencing Project, October 13. Available from: www.sentencingproject.org/reports/the-color-of-justice-racial-and-ethnic-disparity-in-state-prisons-the-sentencing-project/

Nellis, A. 2022. *Nothing But Time: Elderly Americans Serving Life Without Parole*. Washington, DC: The Sentencing Project, June 23. Available from: www.sentencingproject.org/reports/nothing-but-time-elderly-americans-serving-life-without-parole/

Newman, E., D. Newman, & M. Gewirtz. 1984. *Elderly Criminals*. Cambridge, MA: Oelgeschlager, Gunn & Hain.

Newton, N. J. & I. H. Baltys. 2014. 'Parent Status and Generativity in the Context of Race'. *International Jounral of Aging and Human Development*, 78(2), 171–195.

O'Connor, Patricia E. 2000. *Speaking of Crime: Narratives of Prisoners*. Lincoln, NE: University of Nebraska Press.

Office of the Inspector General. 2005. 'Deterring Staff Sexual Abuse of Federal Inmates'. Washington, DC: US Department of Justice.

Owen, B. 1998. *'In the Mix': Struggle and Survival in a Women's Prison*. Albany, NY: State University of New York Press.

Penal Reform International. 2021. *Global Prison Trends 2021: Older Persons*. Available from: www.penalreform.org/global-prison-trends-2021/older-persons/

Pollock, J. 1998. *Counseling Women in Prison*. Thousand Oaks, CA: SAGE.

Pollock, J. 2002. *Women, Prison, and Crime*, 2nd Ed. Belmont, CA: Wadsworth.

Presser, L. 2009. 'The Narratives of Offenders'. *Theoretical Criminology*, 13(2): 177–200.

Prost, S. G., M. A. Novisky, L. Rorvig, N. Zaller, & B. Williams. 2021. 'Prisons and COVID-19: A Desperate Call for Gerontological Expertise in Correctional Health Care'. *Gerontologist*, 6(1): 3–7.

Reed, B. 1985. 'Intervention Strategies for Drug-Dependent Women: An Introduction'. In G. Beschner, G. Reed, & J. Mondanaro, eds., *Treatment Services for Drug-Dependent Women, I*, pp. 1–24. Rockville, MD: National Institute on Drug Abuse.

Reviere, R. & V. Young. 2004. 'Aging Behind Bars: Health Care for Older Women in Prison'. *Journal of Women and Aging*, 16(1–2): 55–67.

Rikard, R. V. & E. Rosenberg. 2007. 'Aging Inmates: A Convergence of Trends in the American Criminal Justice System'. *Journal of Correctional Healthcare*, 13(3): 150–162.

Ross, P. & E. Fabiaro. 1986. *Female Offenders: Correctional Afterthoughts*. Jefferson, NC: McFarland.

Ross, P. & J. Lawrence. 1998. 'Health Care for Women Offenders'. *Corrections Today*, 60(7): 122–129.

Ross, J. & S. Richards. 2002. *Behind Bars: Surviving Prison*. Indianapolis, IN: Alpha Books.

Rowe, J. & R. Kahn. 1998. *Successful Aging*. New York: Pantheon.

Ryff, C. & S. Migdal. 1984. 'Intimacy and Generativity: Self-perceived Transitions'. *Signs*, 9: 470–481.

Sabath, M. & E. Cowles. 1988. 'Factors Affecting the Adjustment of Elderly Inmates in Prison'. In B. McCarthy & R. Langworthy, eds., *Older Offenders: Perspectives in Criminology and Criminal Justice*, pp. 178–195. New York: Praeger.

Sampson, R. & J. Laub. 1992. 'Crime and Deviance in the Life Course'. *Annual Review of Sociology*, 18: 63–84.

Santos, M. 1995. 'Facing Long-Term Imprisonment'. In T. Flanagan, ed., *Long-term Imprisonment*, pp. 36–40. Thousand Oaks, CA: Sage.

Sawyer, W. 2018. *The Gender Divide: Tracking Women's State Prison Growth*. Available from: https://www.prisonpolicy.org/reports/women_overtime.html.

Schoch, D. 2020. 'One in Five Americans Now Provide Unpaid Family Care'. AARP. Available from: www.aarp.org/caregiving/basics/info-2020/unpaid-family-caregivers-report.html

Seidman, I. 1991. *Interviewing as Qualitative Research: A Guide for Researchers in Education and the Social Sciences*. New York: Teachers College Press.

Sentencing Project, The. 2022. *Fact Sheet: Incarcerated Women and Girls*. Washington, DC: The Sentencing Project, May 12. Available from: www.sentencingproject.org/fact-sheet/incarcerated-women-and-girls/

Sharp, S. 2003. 'Mothers in Prison: Issues in Parent-Child Contact'. In S. Sharp and R. Muraskin, eds., *The Incarcerated Woman: Rehabilitative Programming in Women's Prisons*, pp. 151–166. Upper Saddle River, NJ: Prentice Hall.

Sharp, S. & S. Marcus-Mendoza. 2001. 'It's a Family Affair: Incarcerated Women and Their Families'. *Women & Criminal Justice*, 12: 21–49.

Siegal, J. A. 2011. *Disrupted Childhoods: Children of Women in Prison*. New Brunswick, NJ: Rutgers University Press.

Silverstein, M. & E. Litwak. 1993. 'A Task-Specific Typology of Intergenerational Family Structure in Later Life'. *The Gerontologist*, 33: 258–264.

Solares, C., M. Dovrosavljevic, H. Larrson, S. Cortese, & H. Andershed. 2020. 'The Mental and Physical Health of Older Offenders: A Systematic Review and Meta-Analysis'. *Neuroscience & Biobehavioral Reviews*, 119: 440–450.

Sontag, S. 1975. 'The Double Standard of Aging'. In *No Longer Young: The Older Woman in America*. Ann Arbor, MI: Institute of Gerontology.

Stack, C. B. 1974. *All Our Kin: Strategies for Survival in a Black Community*. New York: Harper & Row.

Stolberg, S. 2001. 'Behind Bars, New Efforts to Care for the Dying'. *New York Times*, April 1, p B1.

Suh, A. 2000. 'Military Prostitution in Asia and the United States'. In J. James, ed., *States of Confinement: Policing, Detention, and Prison*, pp. 144–158. New York: St. Martin's Press.

Sykes, G. 1958. *Society of Captives*. Princeton, NJ: Princeton University Press.

Ta, C. 2000. 'Prison Partnership: It's About People'. *Corrections Today*, 62(6): 114–123.

Tasca, M. & J. Turanovic. 2018. *Examining Race and Gender Disparities in Restrictive Housing*. Office of Justice Programs National Criminal Justice Reference Service (NCJRS). Available from: www.ojp.gov/pdffiles1/nij/grants/252062.pdf

Thoits, P. 1995. 'Stress, Coping, and Social Support Processes: Where Are We? What Next'? *Journal of Health and Social Behavior* (Extra Issue), 53–79.

Toch, H. 1975. *Men in Crisis: Human Breakdowns in Prisons*. Chicago, IL: Aldine.

Troll, L. E. 1983. 'Grandparents the Family Watchdog'. In T. H. Brubaker, ed. *Family Relationships in Later Life*, pp. 63–74. Beverly Hills, CA: Sage.

Van Wormer, K. 1981. 'Social Functions of Prison Families: The Feminine Solution'. *Journal of Psychiatry and Law*, 9: 181–191.

Vitucci, J. 1999. 'Inmates With Severe Mental Health Increasing in Jails and Prisons'. *CorrectCare*, 13(1): 4.

Wahidin, A. 2004. *Older Women in the Criminal Justice System: Running Out of Time*. London: Jessica Kingsley.

Walsh, C. 1989. 'The Older and Long Term Inmate Growing Old in the New Jersey Prison System'. *Journal of Offender Counseling, Services and Rehabilitation*, 13: 215–248.

Walsh, C. 1990. 'Needs of Older Inmates in Varying Security Settings'. Unpublished doctoral dissertation. New Brunswick, NJ: Rutgers University Press.

Ward, D. & G. Kassebaum. 1965. *Women, Prison: Sex and Social Structure*. Chicago, IL: Aldine-Atherton.

Watterson, K. 1996. *Women in Prison: Inside the Concrete Womb*, 2nd Ed. Boston, MA: Northeastern University Press.

White, W. 2000. 'The History of Recovered People as Wounded Healers: II. The Era of Professionalization and Specialization'. *Alcoholism Treatment Quarterly*, 18: 1–25.

Wikberg, R. & B. Foster. 1989. 'The Long-Termers: Louisiana's Longest Serving Inmates and Why They've Stayed So Long'. *The Prison Journal*, 80: 9–14.

Williams, V. & M. Fish. 1974. *Convicts, Codes, and Contraband: The Prison Life of Men and Women*. Cambridge, MA: Ballinger.

Yerkes, R. M. 1921. *Psychological Examining in the United States Army: Memoirs of the National Academy of Sciences (Vol. XV)*. Washington, DC: U.S. Government Printing Office.

Young, D. 1998. 'Health Status and Service Use among Incarcerated Women'. *Family and Community Health Journal*, 21: 1–16.

Yurick, A., B. Spier, S. Robb, & N. Ebert, eds. 1984. *The Aged Person and the Nursing Process*, 2nd Ed. Norwalk, CT: Appleton-Century-Crofts.

Zaitzow, B. & A. West. 2003. 'Doing Time in the Shadow of Death: Women Prisoners and HIV/AIDS'. In S. Sharp, ed., *The Incarcerated Woman*, pp. 73–90. Upper Saddle River, NJ: Prentice Hall.

Index

A

abandoned mother 53, 65–70, 104
abnormal sexual behaviour 11
acceptance
   of incarceration 76–78, 88, 104
   of responsibility 78–79, 88, 104, 105
   of self 79–80, 88, 105
active engagement in parenting 45
active psychiatric disorder 33
Aday, R. 29, 31–33, 35–36
Adoption of Safe Families Act 1997 20
'affectional starvation' 14
ageing 1, 27–29, 71
   difficulties associated with physical health 71–72
   encountering disrespect and lack of compassion 72–74
   faith 85–86
   prison
      population 31
      relationships among older women in 83–85
      research specific to 29–30
      shame of 74–75
   three types of acceptance 75–80
   time for self 86–87
   women 2, 3–4
   young and old 80–83
airborne viruses 30
American Association of Retired Persons (AARP) survey 65
American Correctional Association 29
audio-recording devices 47
Azarow, J. 41

B

Babb, S. 31, 35
Bachand, D. 34
Barnett, Rosalind 39
Baro, A. 22
Baruch, Grace 39
Belknap, J. 25
biological children 99–100
Booth, D. 33
Bosworth, M. 24
Brown, J. 44
Bureau of Justice and Statistics 3, 19, 20, 52
Burton, D. 20

C

campus-style housing 33
Chesney-Lind, M. 21
Childhood and Society (Erikson) 37
child sexual abuse 22
chronic conditions 28, 36
chronic health problems 31, 32
chronic medical illness 30
Clemmer, D. 10–13, 16, 71
cognitive dysfunction 28
Colsher, P. 30
community service 43–44, 112
   programmes 103
contented mother 53, 57–61, 69, 70, 104
coping among women in prison 24–25
correctional research endeavours 27
Cowles, E. 35
Cressey, D.R. 12
criminal behaviours 42, 45, 69, 75
criminalization of women 10

D

degenerative arthritic and rheumatic disorders 28
depression 17, 21, 23, 26, 28, 32, 33, 36, 41, 52, 69, 74
de St. Aubin, E. 37, 40, 41, 89
Dholakia, N. 3
Ditton, P. 32
Douglass, R. 30
drug use 20–23, 26

E

Ekstrand, C. 20
Erdman, E. 20
Erikson, E. 2, 8, 39, 42, 89, 90
   Childhood and Society 37
   Gandhi's Truth 38

F

Falter, R. 30
family and friends, relationships with 34–36
feminism 16
feminist perspective, contemporary ethnographies from 16–17
  drug use 20–22
  health care 23–24
  mental health 23
  relational abuse 22–23
  separation from children 18–20
feminist research methods 16
feminist theory 16
Ferraro, K. 24
Fish, M. 25
Foster, B. 35
Fox, J. 25
Freud, Sigmund 38

G

Gandhi's Truth (Erikson) 38
Gannon, L. 28
gender 16, 26
  assimilation of 15
  differences 28
  discrimination and expectations 10
  identity 9
  oppression 7
  stratification 4
Genders, E. 31, 34
generative activities 8, 44, 102
generative behaviours 8, 42, 45, 89, 91, 100, 103, 105, 106
generative programming 105, 106
generativity 2, 8, 36, 37, 89
  expanding on 39–40
  and imprisonment 41–43
  model of 40–41
Giallombardo, Rose 14–15, 75
Gilligan, Carol 39
Girshick, Lori 16–18, 23, 25

H

Halsey, M. 8
Hamm, M. 44
Harris, Jean
  They Always Call Us Ladies 13
Harris, V. 8
Hart, H. 40, 41
health care 18, 23–24, 32, 74
health problems 23, 29–30
  chronic 31, 32
  mental 18
  primary 21
Heffernan, E. 14–16
Henderson, D.J. 21
homosexual relationships 14–16, 84, 85
Human Rights Watch 22

hypertension 30–32
hysterectomies 32

I

impaired cognitive function 28
imprisonment 1–3, 20, 21, 24, 25, 35, 86
  deprivations of 14
  generativity and 41–43
  likelihood and hardship of 8
  prisonization and pains of 10–16
  psychological impact of 45
  for women 18
incarceration 4, 7, 8
  of 'othered' sex 25–26
  traditional research on 10
  woman, legacy of 102–103
institutional drug treatment programmes 23
Institutional Review Board (IRB) 47
'institutional thoughtlessness' 29
intimate-partner abuse 22
'involuntary celibacy' 12
Irwin, J. 12–13, 44

J

Jehl, D. 43

K

Kassebaum, G. 14, 15, 75
Kentucky Department of Corrections (KDOC) 46, 47, 49
Koenig, H. 33
Kratcoski, P. 31, 35
Kreager, D.A. 29

L

Lanier, C. 43
Larson, J.H. 4
Laub, J. 107
Lawrence, J. 23
'least eligibility', principle of 109
LeBel, T. 43
legacy of incarcerated woman 102–103
Loeffelholz, P. 30
Logan, R. 37
lower-income neighbourhoods 4

M

Malloch, M. 21
Mann, C.R. 24
Marcus-Mendoza, S. 19
marginalization 4
Maruna, S. 40–43
McAdams, D. 37, 40–41, 89
McCarthy, M. 34
McClellan, D. 6
mental health 23, 36
  issues 26
  problem 18
mental illness 1, 23, 32, 33, 36, 74

INDEX

mental well-being 28, 29, 32–34
mentoring programmes 106
methodological constraints 49–50
middle adulthood 37, 38
Migdal, S. 39
Millen, D. 6
Miller, D. 21
Moe, A. 24
Morris, A. 23
mother-and-daughter prison
    relationships 97–99
mother-child bond 53, 65

N

Narratives 41
Nation, P. 32, 33, 35, 36
Nelson, J. 4
'New Recovery Movement' 44

O

older women in prison
    cope with incarceration 85
    relationships among 83–85
'othered' sex, incarceration of 25–26
Owen, B. 16–20

P

pains of imprisonment 10–16, 24, 25
parental incarceration 52
parenting 52
    abandoned mother 65–69
    active engagement in 45
    contented mother 57–61
    from prison 44–45
    remorseful mother 53–57
    uneasy mother 61–65
physical health 26–28, 30–32
    difficulties associated with 71–72
    issues 18
physiological deterioration 34
Player, E. 31, 34
poor diet 31
pre-prison socialization experiences 12
primary caregivers 26, 65
prison 101–102
    community 100
    cope with incarceration, older women
        in 85
    environment 16, 33
    experience 3–4, 10–16
    families 24
    mothers and daughters 97–99
    relationships among older women in 83–85
    research specific to ageing in 29–30
    shame of ageing in 74–75
    younger women in 91–97
prison-based rehabilitation programmes 104
prisonization 4, 10–16, 25, 71
pseudo-family groups 14, 16

psychiatric disorder 21, 33
'psycho-sexual' 14

R

Reed, B. 21
relational abuse 22–23, 91
remorseful mother 53–57, 69, 104
reunification 106
Richards, S. 13
Ross, J. 13
Ross, P. 23
Ryff, C. 39

S

Sabath, M. 35
Sales, M. 30
Sampson, R. 107
Santos, M. 34
Sawyer, W. 3
Seidman, I. 47
sentencing laws 1
sentencing reforms 1
Sharp, S. 19
social realities 1, 34
social support 24, 34–36, 108
social system in prison 14
Society of Captives (Sykes) 11
socioemotional selectivity theory 34, 97
Sontag, S. 5
structure generative programming 105
'successful ageing' 29
Suh, A. 74
supportive social network 35
Sykes, Gresham 10, 12, 13, 16
    Society of Captives 11

T

Tasca, M. 8
Tennessee Department of Corrections
    (TDOC) 46
theory of generativity 40, 89
theory of human development 8
They Always Call Us Ladies (Harris) 13
Toch, H. 45
traditional feminine roles 15
Turanovic, J. 8

U

uneasy mother 53, 61–65, 70, 104, 108

V

Vitucci, J. 32

W

Wallace, R. 30
Walsh, C. 33, 34
Ward, David 14, 15, 75
War on Drugs 21
Watterson, K. 20, 25

'weaker sex' 4
Western justice system 89
White, W. 42
Wikberg, R. 35
Williams, V. 25
women
  ageing 2, 3–4
  criminalization of 10
  imprisonment for 18
  in prison
    coping among 24–25
    relationships among older 83–85

Y

Young, D. 32
younger women in prison 59, 89, 91–98, 108

www.ingramcontent.com/pod-product-compliance
Lightning Source LLC
Chambersburg PA
CBHW071716020426
42333CB00017B/2286